Staffordshire Figures

1780–1840

Volume 3

Myrna Schkolne

Schiffer Publishing Ltd

4880 Lower Valley Road • Atglen, PA 19310

Dedication

Dedicated to the memory of Staffordshire's potters, without whom none of this would have happened

Library of Congress Control Number: 2013944801

Cover designed by: Bruce Waters
Type set in Bernhard Modern BT/Arrus BT

ISBN: 978-0-7643-4539-5
Printed in China

Published by Schiffer Publishing, Ltd.
4880 Lower Valley Road
Atglen, PA 19310
Phone: (610) 593-1777; Fax: (610) 593-2002
E-mail: Info@schifferbooks.com

Contents

About Values and Titles.................................... 4

Animal Entertainment
- 111. Performing Animals................................ 5
- 112. Menageries... 11

Animals
- 113. Birds... 16
- 114. Birds with People.................................. 30
- 115. Camels 37
- 116. Cats.. 39
- 117. Cats with People 44
- 118. Cows 46
- 119. Deer 67
- 120. Dogs.. 108
- 121. Dogs with People................................ 129
- 122. Elephants 136
- 123. Foxes 139
- 124. Goats.. 141
- 125. Horses and Donkeys.......................... 145
- 126. Lions, Leopards, Tigers, and Panthers 148
- 127. Mice 175
- 128. Mythical Animals 176
- 129. Other Animals 179
- 130. Rabbits and Hares 183
- 131. Sheep 185
- 132. Squirrels... 238

133. Dandies... 240

Death and Murder
- 134. The Assassination of Marat................ 256
- 135. The Death of Munrow 257
- 136. Menagerie Deaths.............................. 259
- 137. The Red Barn Murder 261

Notes.. 268
Bibliography.. 269
Index 270

About Values and Titles

Values

This work uses the following scale as an approximation of value.

Price A: Up to $1,000 (£625)
Price B: $1,001–$3,000 (£626–£1,875)
Price C: $3,001–$6,000 (£1,876–£3,750)
Price D: $6,001–$9,000 (£3,751–£5,626)
Price E: $9,001–$15,000 (£5,626–£9,375)
Price F: $15,001–$25,000 (£9,376–£15,625
Price G: $25,001 and over (£15,626 and above)

The value of a figure is a function of the standard of its modeling and decoration, its condition, its scarcity, and the appeal of the subject. Essentially, value is quirky, and it can be somewhat subjective. Many small figures are highly desirable and difficult to procure, yet they fall into Price A—even though collectors value them more highly than mediocre figures in higher price brackets.

The determinants of value are not apparent from a photograph, and seemingly identical figures may have vastly different values. The values indicated in captions are not auction values or resale values. Rather, they are the values of figures purchased from a reputable retail source. In each case, the value is an estimate of the value of the figure illustrated. A very similar figure may be worth significantly more or less, depending on the condition and the quality of the glazes and enamels. At the same time, condition issues are not always apparent in a photograph, and, out of respect for those supplying photographs of their treasures for this work, condition reports have not been attached to captions. For that reason, condition is only factored into the value equation to the extent that issues are apparent in the photograph or are known to the author.

Titles

Please note that figure titles are frequently misspelled and have been reproduced in the captions as they appear on the figures.

Animal Entertainment

111. Performing Animals

Long before the days of circuses and traveling menageries, itinerant artistes trudged around Britain with animals whose routines we would be hard-pushed to conceive today. The men who left hearth and home to sleep alongside their beasts with little shelter from the elements were often industrious Italians. Frequently, they rented their animals from Italian providers, often themselves retired itinerant showmen who imported, trained, and leased animals for a livelihood. A "paw-a-piece" alliance was a four-man partnership in bear ownership: two men traveled abroad with a bear and remitted a share of the profits to two domestic sleeping partners. Anything from a porcupine to a troupe of dancing dogs was available for hire at a daily rate, and traveling troupes enabled people across Britain to get a taste of the animal performances that were immensely popular on London stages. These acts must have been picturesque sights, but colorful Staffordshire renditions belie the harshness of the existence that men and animals shared.[1]

All performing animal groups command good prices, but loss of one or another of the small figures from the base impacts value significantly. Groups of a dancing bear and Savoyard are not rare, but they are infrequently on the market. Invariably, the rope tethering the bear is lost or restored. A small lion (in reality a dog dressed in costume) is usually in the foreground, but rarer examples have a monkey. In addition to the examples shown below, a "Sherratt" dancing bear group is documented on a feathered base with triple-oak-leaflet bocage fronds with mayflowers.[2]

Dancing dog troupes are scarcer than dancing bear groups, and again their price reflects their desirability. Troupes of assorted animals (usually a bear, a monkey, and a dog) and their trainers are even harder to find with all animals and the bocage intact. Rarest of all are groups with performing felines.

Figure 111.1. Dancing bear with Savoyard and lion; with bocage. H: 8.5". The small lion in the foreground would have been a dog dressed in a costume with a raffia wig. Note that the Savoyard wears a fur jacket. Price D.

Figure 111.2. Dancing bear with Savoyard and lion, reverse of previous example. The Patriotic Group pot bank frequently used such fronds, but smaller pot banks sometimes used them too.

Figure 111.3. Dancing bear with Savoyard and lion. H: ~8.5". The bocage fronds (but not the flowers) are as on the previous example. Price D. *Moore Collection.*

Figure 111.5. Dancing bear with Savoyard and lion; with bocage. H: 9". Restoration or damage to the rope is almost inevitable because the thumb tends to rest on it when holding the group. Price C.

Figure 111.4. Dancing bear with Savoyard and lion; with bocage. H: 9". The bocage fronds are as on previous examples, but the groups could be from different pot banks. Price D. *Melanie and Nigel Walsh.*

Figure 111.6. Dancing bear with Savoyard and lion; with bocage. H: 8.2". Unusual bocage flowers. As sometimes occurs, the Savoyard wears a fur jacket, in sympathy with his animal friend. Price D.

Figure 111.7. Dancing bear with Savoyard and lion; with bocage. H: 8". The Savoyard's arm was amputated in manufacture. Note the bocage leaves and flowers on the base. Price C. *Richard Montgomery.*

Figure 111.8. Dancing bear with Savoyard and lion; with bocage. Probably attributable to Leather Leaf Group. H: ~8.5". The curled, "leathery" fern leaves are characteristic of this Group, but no other features support attribution. Price C.

Figure 111.9. Dancing bear with Savoyard, dog, and monkey; with bocage. Attributed to Leather Leaf Group. H: 8.3". Some Leather Leaf Group examples are unusual in that they may include a dog and a monkey, rather than a lion. Price D.

Figure 111.10. Dancing bear, reverse of previous example. Bocage leaves were not added to the lower branches. The mottled painting of the base is typical of the Leather Leaf Group.

Figure 111.11. Detail of the monkey and dog on the previous group.

Figure 111.12. Dancing bear with Savoyard and two monkeys; with bocage. H: 8". Two monkeys are most unusual. The generic Salt-type bocage cannot support attribution. Price D. *Jonathan Horne.*

Figure 111.15. Dancing bear with Savoyard, monkey, and dog; with bocage. Attributed to Patriotic Group. H: 9.2". The bocage and base support the attribution. The small animals may be restored. Price B. *Elinor Penna.*

Figure 111.13. Dancing bear with Savoyard and lion; with bocage. Attributed to Patriotic Group. H: 8.8". The bocage flowers are specific to the Group, and tithe pigs from the same pot bank occur on this base. Price C. *Whitehall Antiques, Chapel Hill, North Carolina.*

Figure 111.17. Dancing bear with Savoyard and lion; with bocage. Attributed to Patriotic Group. H: ~8.5". The bocage flowers are exclusive to the Group. Price C.

Figure 111.14. Detail of the previous dancing bear group. *Whitehall Antiques, Chapel Hill, North Carolina.*

Figure 111.16. *WILD MAN & BAIR*. Dancing bear with Savoyard and lion; with bocage. Attributed to Patriotic Group. H: 9". The bocage and base are consistent with the attribution. The titling is also characteristic, but the title tablet is a modern addition, copied from an early example. Price C.

Figure 111.18. Dancing bear with Savoyard; with bocage. H: ~8.8". The bocage fronds are of the common five-leaflet form that occur infrequently on dancing bear groups. Note the colorful plaid jacket and the particularly animated expressions. Price C. *Andrew Dando Antiques.*

Figure 111.19. Dancing bear with Savoyard and lion; with bocage. H: ~8.5". This base also occurs with Flight to Egypt and Return from Egypt groups, and with standing deer. Price B.

Figure 111.20. Dancing bear with Savoyard and lion; with bocage. H: ~8.5". The man and bear are not in their customary positions on the base. Price B.

Figure 111.21. Performing animal troupe. Trainer, organ grinder, dancing bear, and monkey astride dog; with bocage. Attributed to Patriotic Group. H: 5.9", L: 7". All figures are original. The bocage is specific to Patriotic Group. Price C.

Figure 111.22. Performing animal troupe. Organ grinder with monkey astride dog; with bocage. Attributed to Patriotic Group. H: 4.9". Pairs with the following example and known only from this pair. Price D, pair.

Figure 111.24. Performing animal troupe, reverse of previous pair. Flower stalks are integral to the cilantro bocage leaves and are painted to simulate flowers.

Figure 111.23. Performing animal troupe. Trainer with dancing bear; with bocage. Attributed to Patriotic Group. H: 5.2". Pairs with the previous example. The figures are in other animal troupes, but here they are assembled on two bases. Price D, pair.

Figure 111.25. Performing animal troupe. Two trainers, dancing bear, and monkey astride dog; with bocage. H: 6.5". A slightly different base than the preceding and following troupes and lacking an organ grinder. With restoration. Price B.

Figure 111.27. Performing animal troupe. Trainer, organ grinder, dancing bear, and monkey astride dog; with bocage. H: 6.5", L: 7". This common bocage form is rarely found on performing animal troupes. Price B. *Tim Cross, Hastings, England.*

Figure 111.26. Performing animal troupe. Trainer, organ grinder, dancing bear, and monkey astride dog; with bocage. H: 4.6", L: 7". Price B. *Image courtesy of The Potteries Museum & Art Gallery, Stoke-on-Trent, UK.*

Figure 111.28. Performing animal troupe. Trainer, organ grinder, dancing bear, and monkey astride dog; with bocage. L: ~7". The bocage is closely similar to that on the previous example. The hat usually in the trainer's hand is instead in the dog's mouth. Price C. *Jonathan Horne.*

Figure 111.29. Performing animal troupe. Trainer, organ grinder, and dancing bear; with bocage. Possibly made by Hall. H: 6.5". With losses. This base was used by more than one pot bank, but the bocage is suggestive of Hall. Price A. *Collection of Arnold and Barbara Berlin.*

Figure 111.31. *OLD UP IF YOU PLEASE.* Performing animal troupe with trainer, organ grinder, dancing bear, dog, and monkey astride dog; with spill vase. Attributed to "Sherratt". H: 8". The titling, the base, and the painting of the spill vase are typical of "Sherratt." Price D. *Richard Montgomery.*

Figure 111.30. Performing animal troupe. Trainer, organ grinder, dancing bear, and monkey astride dog; with bocage. Attributed to Leaf Mat Group. H: 6". Price B. *Photograph Courtesy of Sotheby's, Inc. © 2014.*

Figure 111.32. Performing animal troupe. Organ grinder, trainer, and dog; with spill vase. Attributed to "Sherratt". The feathered base is specific to "Sherratt." H: 8.1". Price C. © *Christie's Images Limited 2014.*

Figure 111.33. Performing animal troupe. Trainer, organ grinder, and monkey astride dog, within an arbor. H: 5.8". Price D.

Figure 111.34. Exotically attired entertainers and a leopard, with a spill vase. H: 4.9". A rare group known from two examples. Price C.

Figure 111.35. Animal trainer and lions; with bocage. H: 5". Known from only this example. The lions in such groups were, in reality, dogs dressed in costumes that included raffia wigs. The trainer is from the same molds as the organ grinder in the performing animal troupes previously shown. Price C. *Photograph Courtesy of Sotheby's, Inc. © 2014.*

Figure 111.36. Dancing dog troupe. Piper, companion, and three dogs; with bocage. H: ~9". These three-leaflet bocage fronds occur on an unclassified group of figures from the same pot bank. Price D. *John Howard; www.antiquepottery.co.uk.*

Figure 111.37. Dancing dog troupe. Piper, companion, and three dogs; with bocage. H: ~9". The five-leaflet bocage fronds are non-specific. Price D.

Figure 111.38. Dancing dog troupe. Piper, companion, and three dogs; with bocage. H: 8.9". All examples of this troupe are closely similar and probably emanated from the same pot bank. The loss of original dogs diminishes value. Price D.

Figure 111.39. Dancing dog troupe. Piper, companion, and three dogs; with bocage. H: ~9". John Walton used this uncommon bocage on marked figures, but others apparently used it too, and there is no basis for attributing this example. Price D. *Elinor Penna.*

112. Menageries

A menagerie heads many a Staffordshire collector's wish list. These rare objects are the most desirable earthenware groups of their period and command impressive prices. Their whimsical charm and naive coloring and modeling instantly evoke all the excitement of a circus visit in bygone childhood days. Yet nineteenth-century menageries were not circuses. Rather, they were collections of unusual animals whose mere presence was entertainment enough. Menagerie visits did much to dispel long-held beliefs in mythical animals because these creatures failed to appear in menagerie cages.

In the late eighteenth century, the London menagerist Gilbert Pidcock assembled the first sizable traveling menagerie. Customarily, a menagerie set up in the village square. A rectangle was formed, using animal cages for three sides and an elaborate front entrance, bedecked with colorful representations of the animals within, for the fourth. Thomas Frost visited a menagerie in 1825 and recalled, "The display of show-cloths on the outside of this menagerie extended about forty feet in length, and the proprietor's name flamed along the front in coloured lamps." He added that "a brass band of eight performers, wearing scarlet tunics and leopard-skin caps, played on the outside."[1] The menagerie that Frost saw was distinctly similar to the menageries that the Potteries produced: bandsmen in scarlet uniforms, colored lamps, and show cloths portraying immense animals are all found on earthenware menageries.

Several notable menageries toured England in the early 1800s, but only Polito's and Wombwell's menageries are forever captured in clay. George Wombwell was the nineteenth century's ultimate menagerist. By 1805, Wombwell was touring with an impressive array of animals. Traveling menageries were considered educational entertainment, and Wombwell's exhibited for royalty in 1820 and 1834. By 1805, Stephani Polito was also a traveling menagerist, and his caravans accommodated over sixty quadrupeds, including an "Ethiopian savage." Polito's appearance in Wolverhampton, near the Potteries, in 1808[2] possibly inspired the potting of earthenware menageries and their animals in the following decades. Polito died in 1814, but a traveling menagerie lingered under his name until 1835 or 1836, when a storm sank the ship transporting it to Ireland.[3]

The author has recorded the existence of thirty-one menageries, and the smaller menageries are rarer than their larger counterparts. The smallest is the little Wombwell's menagerie in figures 112.1–2. This is also possibly the earliest earthenware menagerie form. It is known from five examples[4] and is the only menagerie that is not attributed to "Sherratt."

"Sherratt" menageries are very different from the little Wombwell's menagerie, and they are significantly larger. Examples are titled to represent both Polito's and Wombwell's menageries. All can be confidently attributed to "Sherratt" because all stand on bases that are only associated with "Sherratt." Also, some of the smaller figures on menagerie platforms occur as individual figures, always on bases used only by "Sherratt." There appears to have been a sequential progression in the manufacture of "Sherratt" menageries.

1. **Small Polito's menagerie** (figs. 112.3–4). This menagerie is constructed around a plate fronting a three-dimensional house-like structure that sits atop a table base. The mass of this structure is impressive, and large holes were cut in it to allow for ventilation during firing. Titling is always on a scroll that goes around the sides and top of the front plate. The menagerie is about thirteen inches high and is recorded on only clawed table bases (in one case painted yellow rather than the usual brown). Clawed bases do not occur on "Sherratt" groups that can be dated to after 1830. Thus, "Sherratt" Tam O'Shanter and Souter Johnny, Tee Total, and Ale Bench (all dating from 1828) never have clawed bases. Only seven examples of this menagerie are recorded.

2. **Large Polito's menagerie** (figs. 112.5–9). This menagerie is constructed in the same manner as the smaller Polito's menagerie, and it uses the same front plate. However, it is assembled on a base that is about 3.5" longer. The overall height remains about 13" when on a table base (as is usually the case), but the menagerie platform is longer. The longer platform accommodates additional figures, and one example (fig. 112.9) has two tall gaslights added to either end of the platform. Figures at the ends of the longer menagerie platform may be lost, and loss or replacement impacts value. Some examples also have figures on the steps leading to the platform, and these are frequently damaged, lost, or restored. As with all menageries, restoration to the animals perched atop is considered inevitable. This large Polito's is by far the most common of the "Sherratt" menageries, and it occurs on a range of bases, including brown clawed bases. Fourteen examples are recorded.

3. **Large Wombwell's menagerie, constructed like Polito's** (figs. 112.10–11). This menagerie is an adaptation of the large Polito's and is made in the same form, with a house-like structure atop a base. It uses the front plate used for all Polito's menageries and is on a clawed table base. Titling is in a similar manner, but WOMBWELL (without the "S") is squeezed into the spot that previously accommodated POLITOS. Only one example is recorded: a large menagerie in the Willett Collection was made in this manner, and it is apparent that less effort was expended on decorating. Whereas the backs and sides of Polito's menageries are extensively decorated, no enamel colors were applied to the back, base, or sides of the Willett's large Wombwell's. This simplification implies cost reduction, that, when considered in conjunction with the evolution of menagerie forms, suggests that this large Wombwell's was introduced after the large Polito's.

4. **Large Wombwell's with a modified back plate** (figs. 112.12–16). Other examples of Wombwell's menageries show cost-reduction taken further. Here the front plate has been refashioned and its titled scroll has been removed. Titling is confined to *WOMBWELLS MENAGERIE* (note that the "S" has been added back into the title) added near the center of the front plate. Significantly, the house-like support for the front plate is absent; instead the front plate stands alone as a simple slab of clay. "Sherratt" made these simpler menageries on bases of two lengths, as was done with Polito's menageries. None of these modified Wombwell's menageries stands on a clawed table base, and all are believed to postdate more elaborate forms. Four examples are recorded.

Figure 112.1. *THE LARGEST COLLECTION OF ANIMALS WOMBWELL S IMMENSE MENAGERIE OF WILD BEASTS &C.* H: 8.5". The menagerie plate fronts an open box-like structure, possibly a spill holder. This is the only form of menagerie not attributed to "Sherratt." Price G.

Figure 112.3. *POLITOS ROYAL MENAGERIE OF THE WONDERFULL BURD AND BEASTS FROM MOST PARTS OF THE WORLD LION &C.* Attributed to "Sherratt." H: 13", L: 9". This small Polito's is rarer than larger Polito's and, because recorded examples only occur on clawed bases, probably earlier. Price G.

Figure 112.4. Polito's Menagerie, previous example, showing the structure and large vent holes beneath.

Figure 112.2. Wombwell's Menagerie, previous example, open on the top to serve as a spill holder.

Figure 112.5. *POLITOS ROYAL MENAGERIE OF THE WONDERFULL BURDS AND BEASTS FROM MOST PARTS OF THE WORLD LION &C.* Attributed to "Sherratt." H: 12.6", L~13". This is the larger Polito's. It is longer than figure 112.3, but the height is the same. Price G. *Waddington's, Toronto.*

Figure 112.6. *POLITOS ROYAL MERAGERIE OF THE WONDERFULL BURDS AND BEASTS FROM MOST PARTS OF THE WORLD LION &C.* Attributed to "Sherratt." H: 13.2"; L: 12.6". Placement of characters on menagerie steps and platforms may vary. Price G. *Collection of Arnold and Barbara Berlin.*

Figure 112.7. *POLITOS MENAGERIE OF THE WONDERFULL BURDS AND BEASTS FROM MOST PARTS OF THE WORLD LION &C.* Attributed to "Sherratt." H: 13.3, L: ~13". The man on the right is unusual and does not appear on other menageries. The lady on the steps may be from the same molds as Maria Marten on "Sherratt" Red Barn Groups. Price G. © *Fitzwilliam Museum, Cambridge.*

Figure 112.8. *POLITOS ROYAL MENAGERIE OF THE WONDERFULL BURDS AND BEASTS FROM MOST PARTS OF THE WORLD LION &C.* Attributed to "Sherratt." H: 11.8". Price G. *Jonnys Antiques.*

Figure 112.9. *POLITIS ROYAR MENAGERIE OF THE WONDERFULL BURDS AND BEASTS FROM MOST PARTS OF THE WORLD LION &C.* Attributed to "Sherratt." H: 13". Note the tall gaslights placed to either side. Price G. The *Moore Collection.*

Figure 112.12. *WOMBWELLS MENAGERIE.* Attributed to "Sherratt." H: 14.5", L: ~13". About the length of a large Polito's menagerie. The house-like structure and elaborate titling evident in the previous examples are not used. Price G. *Elinor Penna.*

Figure 112.10. *WOMBWELL ROYAL MENAGERIE OF THE WONDERFULL BURDS AND BEASTS FROM MOST PARTS OF THE WORLD LION &C.* Attributed to "Sherratt." H: 11". The front plate is beautifully painted, but the base and back are undecorated. The feet, now lost, were clawed. Price G. *Brighton and Hove Museums.*

Figure 112.13. Wombwell's Menagerie, side of previous example. Unlike on previously shown menageries, the plate stands as a simple slab. *Elinor Penna.*

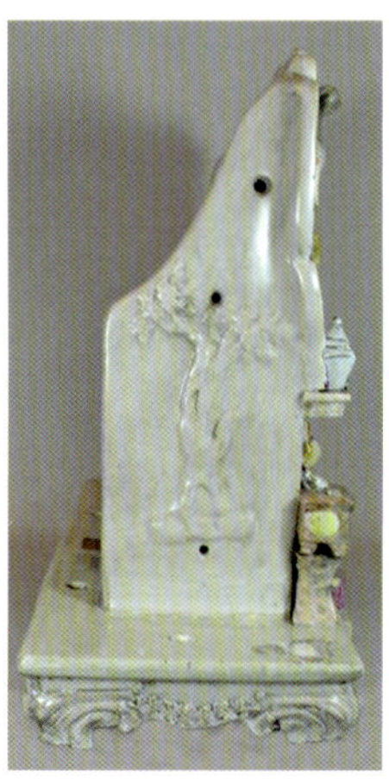

Figure 112.11. Wombwell's Menagerie, previous example. A house-like structure stands atop the platform. Note the very many vent holes cut in it. *Brighton and Hove Museums.*

Figure 112.14. *WOMBWELLS MENAGERIE.* Attributed to "Sherratt." H: 12.8". Simplified, lacking the house-like support for the front plate and the titled scroll. Not as long, being comparable in length to the smaller Polito's menagerie. Price G.

Figure 112.15. *WOMBWELLS MENAGERIE.* Attributed to "Sherratt." H: 14.7", L: 13". This is essentially a longer version of the previous menagerie, the added length accommodating an additional character on the right end of the platform. Price G. *The William Herbert and Nancy Hunt Collection.*

Figure 112.16. *WOMBWELLS MENAGERIE.* Attributed to "Sherratt." H: 14.7", L: 13". Like the previous menagerie but the wall to the right of the door is not present, allowing space for an additional musician on the platform. Note the monkeys perched to the sides. Price G. *The William Herbert and Nancy Hunt Collection.*

Animals

113. Birds

From the late eighteenth century, there was widespread interest in natural history. In keeping with that sentiment, wealthy gentlemen stocked aviaries on their estates with birds of exotic plumage, and ladies enjoyed exquisite mechanical automata that trilled on demand. Earthenware birds were popular decorations and came in all shapes and sizes, ranging from small whistles to imposing cockerels.

Figure 113.1. Dovecote. Incised "M.S. 1824" beneath. H: 10.1". Motifs of embracing children and cooing love birds suggest the dovecote was a love token. Price G. *Collection of Arnold and Barbara Berlin.*

Figure 113.2. Dovecote, previous example. The motifs on the side also occur as separate figures (Vol. 4, figs. 197.80–81). The motif on the reverse portrays the struggle between the brothers Eros and Anteros (Vol. 4, 197.1–8). *Collection of Arnold and Barbara Berlin.*

Figure 113.3. Whistle, with canary. H: 2.1". After a similar Derby whistle, circa 1780. Price A.

Figure 113.4. Whistle, with bird. Attributed to Dudson. H: 2.8". Price B. *Image courtesy of The Potteries Museum & Art Gallery, Stoke-on-Trent, UK.*

Figure 113.5. Detail of the x-sprig on the base of the previous figure. This distinctive sprig is specific to Dudson. *Image courtesy of The Potteries Museum & Art Gallery, Stoke-on-Trent, UK.*

Figure 113.6. Whistle, with cockerel. H: 3.5". Pairs with the following whistle. Price B. © *Victoria and Albert Museum, London.*

Figure 113.7. Whistle, with hen. H: 3.5". Pairs with the preceding whistle. Price B. *John Howard; www.antiquepottery.co.uk.*

Figure 113.8. Whistle, with cockerel. H: ~3". Price A.

Figure 113.9. Whistle, with goldfinch. H: ~3". After a similar Derby bird, circa 1760. Price B. *John Howard; www.antiquepottery.co.uk.*

Figure 113.10. Whistle, with songbird. H: ~2.5". Price B.

Figure 113.11. Bird-shaped whistle. Possibly attributable to "Sherratt". H: 1.7". "Sherratt" used similar leafy patterns on the green bases of some small figures. Price A. *Martyn Edgell Antiques Ltd.*

Figure 113.12. Pair of small songbirds. H: 2.8". A rare pair that commands a price premium. Price C. *Phil Masters Antiques, Leek.*

Figure 113.13. Goldfinch. H: 3.4". After a similar Derby bird, circa 1760. Price A. *Andrew Dando Antiques.*

Figure 113.14. Goldfinch. H: ~2". Like the previous example, probably after the Derby figure. Price A.

Figure 113.15. Songbird. H: ~2". Price A.

Figure 113.16. Bird with exotic plumage. H: ~3". Price A.

Figure 113.17. Songbird. H: ~3". Price A. *Andrew Dando Antiques.*

Figure 113.18. Songbird on a perch simulating carved wood. H: ~10". Note the size. Known from only this example. Price B. *Andrew Dando Antiques.*

Figure 113.19. Parrot. H: 6.5". In the style of earlier Chinese porcelain birds. Price B. *John Howard; www.antiquepottery.co.uk.*

113.20. Bird, possibly a partridge. H: ~3". Price A.

113.21. Small bird with a nest of eggs. H: 2.7". Price A.

113.22. Owl. H: ~12". Small owls occur as components of larger groups, but this is the only recorded example of an owl as a lone figure. Price C.

Figure 113.23. Swan, its head resting on its breast. H: 7". Price B. *John Howard; www.antiquepottery.co.uk.*

Figure 113.24. Swan forming the knob to the lid of a box on raised feet with lion mask handles. H: 5.5". Price C. *Doyle New York.*

Figure 113.26. Pair of peacocks. Probably made by Hall. H: 4". Two peacocks (rather than a peacock and peahen) frequently occur paired. The flowers visible on the base of the right hand peacock suggest a "Hall" attribution. Price B.

Figure 113.25. Turkey. Probably made by Hall. H: 4.5". The six-petalled flowers on the base suggest a "Hall" attribution. Price B. *The William Herbert and Nancy Hunt Collection.*

Figure 113.27. Pair of peacocks. Probably made by Hall. H: 4". Like the previous peacocks. Here the flowers on the bases are painted in a manner very suggestive of Hall. Price B. *Michael Goodacre.*

Figure 113.28. Pair of peacocks. H: 4". Price B.

Figure 113.29. Peacock. H: 4". The base and its decoration are in the style of Enoch Wood. Price A.

Figure 113.30. Peacock and base excavated from a site associated with Enoch Wood. Other pot banks also made peacocks from closely similar molds. *Image courtesy of The Potteries Museum & Art Gallery, Stoke-on-Trent, UK.*

Figure 113.31. Peacock. H: 4.5". Like previous peacocks, but the decoration on the base suggests manufacture by a different pot bank. Price A. *Brighton and Hove Museums.*

Figure 113.32. Peacock and peahen, a pair. H: ~4"(L), ~3.8"(R.) No other example of a peahen is recorded. Price B.

Figure 113.33. Peacock. H: ~3.9". Price A.

Figure 113.34. Eagle. H: 8". Attributed to Enoch Wood/Wood & Caldwell. A large flower specific to this pot bank is on the front of the mound beneath the eagle. Price B. © *Victoria and Albert Museum, London.*

Figure 113.35. Eagle. H: 8". Price B. *Martyn Edgell Antiques Ltd.*

Figure 113.36. Eagle. Probably made by Enoch Wood/Wood & Caldwell. H: 8.3". The base suggests the attribution. However, a similar eagle on this base and impressed "WEDGWOOD" has been documented. Price B. *Image courtesy of The Potteries Museum & Art Gallery, Stoke-on-Trent, UK.*

Figure 113.37. The base of the previous figure. *Image courtesy of The Potteries Museum & Art Gallery, Stoke-on-Trent, UK.*

Figure 113.38. Eagle atop an inkwell with dolphins. H: 6". The dolphins' open mouths form quill rests. The shells to either side are water reservoirs for cleaning nibs. The central shell is fed by a hole in the bird and is for ink. Price B. *Collection of Arnold and Barbara Berlin.*

Figure 113.39. Eagle upon an inkwell with dolphins. H: 6". Price B. *Steve Cook.*

Figure 113.40. Eagle. H: 2.8". Price A. *www. madelena.com.*

Figure 113.41. Pair of pheasant tureens. H: 4.5", L: 6.5". Price C. *The William Herbert and Nancy Hunt Collection.*

Figure 113.42. Nun pigeon tureen. L: ~6.5". The nun pigeon is the oldest pigeon breed, and its hood of feathers gives the breed its name. Price B. *John Howard; www.antiquepottery.co.uk.*

Figure 113.43. Nun pigeon. L: ~6.5". Unusual in that a fledgling nestles close to its mother. Unlike the previous example, it is not a tureen and is open beneath. Price B. *Andrew Dando Antiques.*

Figure 113.44. Nun pigeon with fledgling. H: 4", L: 6". Companion to the following pigeon. Both are decorative and do not serve as tureens. Price B, pair. *The William Herbert and Nancy Hunt Collection.*

Figure 113.45. Nun pigeon. H: 4", L: 6". Companion to the previous pigeon but, unlike it, does not have a fledgling. Price B, pair. *The William Herbert and Nancy Hunt Collection.*

Figure 113.46. Pair of nun pigeon tureens and a pair of closely similar smaller nun pigeons. H: 4.5", L: 7" and H: 2.5", L 4". Price C. *Jonnys Antiques.*

Figure 113.47. Pair of game fowl. H: 8.2". These rare fowl also occur decorated in under-glaze colors. Price C. *Andrew Dando Antiques.*

Figure 113.49. Cockerel with detachable head. H: 9.8". Like the previous cockerel, but the plumage is painted differently. Price C. *John Howard; www.antiquepottery.co.uk.*

Figure 113.48. Pair of cockerels with detachable heads. H: 8.3". Cockerels with detachable heads are after eighteenth-century Asian porcelain cockerels that possibly served as incense burners. Price E. *Philip Carrol.*

Figure 113.50. Cockerel. H: 10". The head of this bird is not removable, but the figure is otherwise very like those with detachable heads. Price C. *John Howard; www.antiquepottery.co.uk.*

Figure 113.51. Cockerel. H: 9.2". The decoration of the base is most unusual. Price C. *John Howard; www.antiquepottery.co.uk.*

Figure 113.52. Cockerel with detachable head. H: ~9". Price C.

Figure 113.53. Cockerel. H: 8.5". Price C. *John Howard; www.antiquepottery.co.uk.*

Figure 113.54. Cockerel. H: 8.5". Differs from previous cockerels in that both legs are integral to the base. Price C. *Andrew Dando Antiques.*

Figure 113.55. Cockerel. Probably made by the Scottish east coast potteries. H: 8". Decorated in under-glaze colors with some enamel in a color palette suggesting a Scottish origin. Price C. *John Howard; www.antiquepottery.co.uk.*

Figure 113.56. Cockerel. H: 3.6". Cockerels of a smaller size inevitably have both legs integral to the base. Price A. *Andrew Dando Antiques.*

Figure 113.57. Cockerel. H: 4.2". Price A. *Andrew Dando Antiques.*

Figure 113.58. Cockerel. H: 4.3". Price A. *Aurea Carter Antiques.*

Figure 113.59. Hen. H: 3". Price A. *John Howard; www.antiquepottery.co.uk.*

Figure 113.60. Cockerel. H: ~3". Possibly a companion to the following hen. Price A.

Figure 113.61. Hen. H: ~2.8". Possibly a companion to the previous cockerel. Price A.

Figure 113.62. Hen with chicks; with bocage. H: ~4.5". Chicks and a water bowl are integral to the base. Price B. *John Howard; www. antiquepottery.co.uk.*

Figure 113.63. Pair of spill vases, large canaries perched in branches to either side of each vase. Attributed to "Sherratt." H: 5.5". The bocages and floral sprigs applied to the bases support attribution. The bocage flowers are decorated in pink luster, as sometimes occurs only on "Sherratt" figures. Price C. *John Howard; www. antiquepottery.co.uk.*

Figure 113.64. Spill vase with two large canaries perched in branches. Attributed to "Sherratt." H: 5.7". Price B.

Figure 113.65. Spill vase with two large canaries perched in branches. Attributed to "Sherratt." H: 5.5". Price B.

Figure 113.66. Spill vase with exotic birds perched atop and four sheep on the base. H: 6.8". Price B. *Martyn Edgell Antiques Ltd.*

Figure 113.67. Detail of the previous spill vase. A ball of clay atop the sheep's back is not present on other similar vases. *Martyn Edgell Antiques Ltd.*

Figure 113.68. Spill vase with exotic birds perched atop and four sheep on the base. H: 6.3". From the same molds as the previous spill vase, but leaves and a flower (painted green) are at the birds' feet and on the base. Price B. *Andrew Dando Antiques.*

Figure 113.69. Two oversized canaries within a bocage tree. H: ~9". Restoration to the bocage. A similarly styled group includes a man perched atop the tree (Vol. 4, fig. 147.51). Price B.

Figure 113.71. Bird in a tree; with bocage. H: ~7". Price A.

Figure 113.70. Birds in a tree with a nest; with bocage. H: 8.7". A very unusual bocage comprising bocage leaves of two forms. Price B. *Melanie and Nigel Walsh.*

Figure 113.72. Bird on a naturalistic stump; with bocage. H: ~5". Four tiny fledglings are integral to the base. Price A.

Figure 113.73. Pheasants; with bocage. Impressed "WALTON". H: ~3". Forms part of a six-piece hunting garniture made by John Walton. With restoration to the birds and bocage. Price B.

Figure 113.74. Birds with shells before a bocage. H: ~6". The bocage may represent seaweed and only otherwise occurs on similarly styled figures of a child collecting shells (Vol. 4, figs. 199.22–24). Price B.

114. Birds with People

People have always enjoyed the beauty of birds, and earthenware figures of ladies with songbirds and couples feeding farmyard chickens recall the pleasures of a bygone era. Some of the earliest figures and groups depicting birds were made by Ralph Wood in the late eighteenth century. Of note is an enamel-painted figure of a girl holding a large bird, attributed to Ralph Wood and impressed "87". Only one example is known and it is not shown here. An unpainted example of this figure impressed "Ra. Wood Burslem" and "87" is in the collection of Colonial Williamsburg (1963.332).

Far better known is the group of a lady holding a bird and a man holding a birdcage, first made by Ralph Wood (figs. 114.1–3) and then Dudson (figs. 114.4–5). The grouping is allegorical of liberty and matrimony, and Ralph Wood examples may be impressed "89" or "90". Bow and Derby made porcelain interpretations of this theme from the 1750s, after Joachim Kaendler's Meissen prototypes of 1750–1752. The inspiration for the Meissen groups is thought to be the theme of the conflict between liberty and matrimony, as captured by Nicolas Lancret (1690–1743) in a painting showing a youth holding a bird while his lady holds an empty birdcage. However, these porcelain renditions were modeled as two separate figures—he with a bird aloft, she with an empty bird cage.

Figures showing the pastime of bird nesting are shown in Volume 4, chapter 147.

Figure 114.1. Liberty and Matrimony. Man holding birdcage, lady holding bird; with bocage. Attributed to Ralph Wood. H: 10.9". Also recorded impressed "89" or "90". A color-glazed example marked "Ra. Wood Burslem" has been documented, as has a porcelain example attributed to Ralph Wood. Price B. © *Victoria and Albert Museum, London.*

Figure 114.2. Liberty and Matrimony. Man holding birdcage, lady holding bird, with candle holder; with bocage. Attributed to Ralph Wood. H: 11". This group occurs titled Bird-catchers. Companion to a shepherd musicians group that is sometimes impressed "89" or "90" and sometimes includes a candle holder (Vol. 1, fig. 26.160). Price B.

Figure 114.3. Liberty and Matrimony. Man holding birdcage, lady holding bird; with bocage. Attributed to Ralph Wood. H: 11". Companion to fig. 26.163 (Vol. 1). Price B. *Image courtesy of The Potteries Museum & Art Gallery, Stoke-on-Trent, UK.*

Figure 114.4. *Bird Catchers*, Liberty and Matrimony. Man holding birdcage, lady holding bird; with bocage. Attributed to Dudson. H: 12.8". The bocage and titling are typical of Dudson. Dudson groups postdate Ralph Wood groups, which can also occur on square bases with this title. Price B.

Figure 114.5. *Bird catcher*, Liberty and Matrimony. Man holding birdcage, lady holding bird; with bocage. Attributed to Dudson. H: ~13". Like the previous group but with a different Dudson bocage. Figure 26.166 (Vol. 1) is the companion to this model. Price B.

Figure 114.6. & *Partner*. Girl holding goose. Attributed to Ralph Wood; impressed "136". H: 9.5". Perhaps intended to pair with Ralph Wood's *Falconer*, which occurs impressed "135" (Vol. 2, fig. 84.80). Price A. *Image courtesy of The Potteries Museum & Art Gallery, Stoke-on-Trent, UK.*

Figure 114.7. & *Partner*, reverse of previous figure showing "136" impressed on the back of the base. *Image courtesy of The Potteries Museum & Art Gallery, Stoke-on-Trent, UK.*

Figure 114.8. Girl with parrot. H: 8.2". Pairs with a boy crying (Vol. 4, fig. 145.4). Price A. *Brighton and Hove Museums.*

Figure 114.9. Girl with parrot. H: 6.6". Price A. *Aurea Carter Antiques.*

Figure 114.10. Girl with parrot, boy with cockerel, a pair. H: 6.6". Price B.

Figure 114.11. Boy with bird; with bocage. H: ~5.6". Price A. *Bamfords Auctioneers and Valuers Ltd.*

Figure 114.12. Boy with goose. H: 5.2". The color palette is typical of that on late eighteenth-century figures. Price A.

Figure 114.13. Boy with goose. H: 7". This figure is much larger than the previous example. Price A. *Elinor Penna.*

Figure 114.14. Boy with bird. H: 4.4". Price A.

Figure 114.15. Boy with bird, girl with bird, an assembled pair. H: 4.4"(L), 4.2"(R). Price A.

Figure 114.16. Girl with parrot. H: 4.7". Price A.

Figure 114.17. Girl with parrot. H: 4.7". Like the previous figure, but differences in enameling impart great individuality. Price A. *Nick Burton.*

Figure 114.18. Girl with bird. H: ~5.3". Pairs with figure 147.24 (Vol. 4) and is rarer than her partner. Price A.

Figure 114.19. Boy with bird. H: 5". Unlike other boys with birds, this boy is attired in classical garb. An uncommon figure. Price A. *Martyn Edgell Antiques Ltd.*

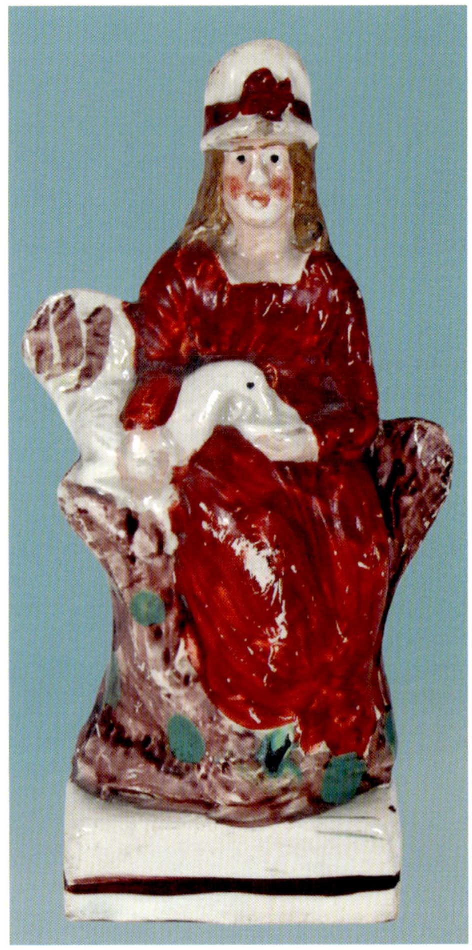

Figure 114.20. Woman with cockerel. H: 4.4". Price A. *Brighton and Hove Museums.*

Figure 114.21. Girl feeding chickens; with bocage. H: 6.3". These three-leaflet bocage fronds also occur on other related figures awaiting classification. Price A.

Figure 114.22. Boy feeding chicken; with bocage. H: 6.2". Bocage restored. Price A.

Figure 114.23. Man and woman with birds, nest, and dog; with bocage. H: ~6". Price A.

Figure 114.24. Man and woman with birds, nest, and goat (or dog); with bocage. H: ~6". Price A.

Figure 114.25. Man and woman with birds, nest, and sheep; with bocage. H: 6.1". Price A.

Figure 114.26. Man, woman with chicken, and boy with nest; with bocage. H: 8.4". An unusual conglomeration of figures assembled to form a possibly unique group. All figures are original to the base. Price A. *Brighton and Hove Museums.*

Figure 114.27. *Cock-Fighters*. Man, woman holding cockerel, with two cockerels; with bocage. Attributed to Ralph Wood. H: ~8.7". The titling of the base is typical of Ralph Wood, as is the painting of the line that extends around three sides only. Bocage restored. Cock fighting was banned in 1849. Price A.

Figure 114.28. Man, woman holding cockerel, with two cockerels; with bocage. Attributed to Dudson. H: 9.4". A similar group titled *Cock Fanciers* is recorded. Price B. *Elinor Penna.*

Figure 114.29. Man, woman holding cockerel, with two cockerels; with bocage. Attributed to Dudson. H: ~9". The bocage supports the attribution. Price B.

Figure 114.30. Man, woman holding cockerel, with two cockerels, bocage lost. H: 9.3". Price A. *Photograph Courtesy of Sotheby's, Inc. © 2014.*

Figure 114.31. Man, woman holding cockerel, with two cockerels; with bocage. H: 9.2". Note her attractive hat. Price C.

Figure 114.32. Reverse of previous example. The bocage leaves are flat on the back, i.e. each leaf has not been paired back-to-back with another.

Figure 114.33. Man with cockerel, woman feeding hen and chickens; with bocage. Impressed "WALTON". H: ~7.5". Price B.

Figure 114.34. Man with cockerel, woman feeding hen and chickens; with bocage. Impressed "WALTON". H: ~7.5". Price B. *Andrew Dando Antiques.*

115. Camels

In the early nineteenth century, a camel was an uncommon sight in England, and earthenware camels are correspondingly elusive. Although the Royal Menagerie had owned a camel as early as the thirteenth century, by 1810, only one camel existed in England[1] because camels did not fare well in England's climate. In 1829, James Rennie noted that the one-humped dromedary or Arabian camel was often exhibited on the streets of large cities, but England's climate shortened its life span.[2] Of the two-humped Bactrian camel Rennie wrote, "there is a camel with two humps daily led about the streets of London.... Indeed this species appears fitted by nature for a moister atmosphere than the Arabian camel, and may thus be somewhat adapted to our country. In the winter this camel is wrapped up, and has sometimes a fire in his stable, if the weather is particularly cold."[3]

Recorded but not shown is a small camel with bocage that is attributed to John Dale.

Figure 115.1. Dromedary and Bactrian camels, a pair; with spill holders. . H: 5.5"(L), 6"(R). The dromedary is painted "18" beneath. Price C. *Image courtesy of The Potteries Museum & Art Gallery, Stoke-on-Trent, UK.*

Figure 115.2. Bactrian camel, to the left, bocage lost. H: 5". Price A.

Figure 115.3. Bactrian camel, to the left; with bocage. H: 7". Price C. *The William Herbert and Nancy Hunt Collection.*

Figure 115.4. Dromedary, to the right; with bocage. H: 7.5". Price C.

Figure 115.5. Bactrian camel, to the left; with bocage. H: 7.1". Price C.

Figure 115.6. Dromedary, to the right; with bocage. H: ~8". Price C.

Figure 115.7. Bactrian camel, to the left; with bocage. H: 8". Price D. *John Howard; www.antiquepottery.co.uk.*

Figure 115.8. Bactrian camel, reverse of previous figure, with flowers on the back of the bocage. *John Howard; www.antiquepottery.co.uk.*

116. Cats

In the early nineteenth century, the cat was not yet fully established as a domestic companion, and cats lacked the status of other pedigreed animals. In parts of the country, the cat was still associated with witchcraft, and centuries-old practices of persecuting cats for pleasure continued. England's first animal cruelty legislation, enacted in 1822, did not protect cats and other domestic animals. That figures of cats are much rarer than figures of dogs reflects contemporary societal preferences.

Figure 116.1. Cat, a mouse in its mouth, another mouse peering down a hole in the base. L: ~8.2". The base simulates a brick floor. Known from only this and the following figure. Price E. *Newcastle-under-Lyme Museum.*

Figure 116.2. Cat with mice, previous figure from beneath. *Newcastle-under-Lyme Museum.*

Figure 116.3. Cat, a mouse in its mouth, a mouse hole in the base. L: 8.2". This group was made with only one mouse. The base again simulates a brick floor but differs in form from the base of the previous example. Price E. *Nick Burton.*

Figure 116.4. Large seated tabby cat. Attributed to Copeland & Garrett. H: 14.4". The attribution is based on a reliable source recalling a very similar marked example. Price E. *Bonhams.*

Figure 116.5. Large seated marmalade cat. Attributed to Copeland & Garrett. H: ~14.4". Like the previous cat but painted differently. Price E. *John Howard; www.antiquepottery.co.uk.*

Figure 116.6. Large seated cat with a sponged coat. H: ~9". Price D. *John Howard; www.antiquepottery.co.uk.*

Figure 116.7. Large seated spotted cat. H: ~9". Price D. *John Howard; www.antiquepottery.co.uk.*

Figure 116.8. Cat with a mottled coat, seated to the right. H: 4.5". Price C. *Saffron Walden Museum.*

Figure 116.9. Cat with a marmalade coat, seated to the left. H: 4.5". Price C.

Figure 116.10. Cat with an exotically painted coat, seated to the left. H: 3.5". Unlike previous cats, this one has its base integral to the body. Price A. *Leatherwood Antiques, leatherwoodantiques.com.*

Figure 116.11. Cat, seated to the right. H: 2.8". Price A. *The Bowes Museum, Barnard Castle.*

Figure 116.12. Cat, seated to the right. H: 2.8". The black is enamel, and the other colors are under the glaze. Price B. *John Howard; www.antiquepottery.co.uk.*

Figure 116.13. Cat, seated to the left. Attributed to "Sherratt." H: 2.1". Similarly styled dogs are also from this pot bank. These teeny, charming figures are treasured for their naiveté. Price A.

Figure 116.14. Cat, recumbent to the left; with bocage. Attributed to Leaf Mat Group. H: 2.6". Price B.

Figure 116.15. Cat, recumbent to the left. Probably attributable to Leaf Mat Group. H: 2.2". Made without a bocage but from the same molds as the previous cat, both having the same distinctive motif on their bases. Price B. *Andrew Dando Antiques.*

Figure 116.16. Cat, recumbent to the left. L ~2.5". Price B.

Figure 116.17. Cat, recumbent to the right. L: ~2.5". Small dogs occur on similar pillow-shaped bases. Price B. *John Howard; www.antiquepottery.co.uk.*

Figure 116.18. Cat, recumbent to the right. L: ~2.5". Price B. *John Howard; www.antiquepottery.co.uk.*

Figure 116.19. Cat, recumbent to the right. L: ~2.9". Price B. *John Howard; www.antiquepottery.co.uk.*

Figure 116.20. Cat, recumbent to the right. L: ~2.9". Like the previous cat, but differences in decoration impart great individuality. Price B. *John Howard; www.antiquepottery.co.uk.*

Figure 116.21. Cat, recumbent to the right. L: ~2.9". This model cat is recorded on a base painted with blue rather than pink and paired with a mouse. Mice are even rarer than cats. Price B. *John Howard; www.antiquepottery.co.uk.*

Figure 116.22. Cat, recumbent to the right. L: 2.4". This cat pairs with a mouse (fig. 127.1). The mouse is on a longer base than the cat, the extra length being needed to accommodate its tail. Price B.

Figure 116.23. Cat seated alongside a dog; with bocage. Height not known. A rare group known from only this example. Price B.

117. Cats with People

Early earthenware cats are rare as stand-alone figures, and even fewer models show a cat in the arms of its owner. Some figures of a girl holding her cat pair with a boy with his dog, and such figures evidence the dawning equality between the two species within English homes.

Figure 117.1. Boy with a dog, girl holding a cat, a pair. H: 7.9"(L), 8.1"(R). An uncommon pairing, as figures of girls holding cats usually are found alone. Price B. *Brighton and Hove Museums.*

Figure 117.2. Girl holding a cat. H: 8.4". From the same molds as figure 117.1. The blue line banding the base is very uncommon. A similarly modeled unpainted pearlware figure of a girl holding a bird is impressed "Ra. Wood Burslem" and "87" (Colonial Williamsburg 1963.332). Price A. *Richard Montgomery.*

Figure 117.3. Girl holding a cat. H: 6.4". From slightly different molds from the preceding girl. The color palette suggests late eighteenth-century manufacture. Pairs with a boy with dog (fig. 121.10). Price A.

Figure 117.4. Girl holding a cat. H: 6.1". Like the previous figure but made without a hat atop the cap. A figure like this is recorded paired with a boy with a dog (fig. 121.8). Price A.

Figure 117.5. Girl seated holding a cat. H: 3.1". Price A. *Aurea Carter Antiques.*

118. Cows

In the early eighteenth century, cattle were valued primarily as draught animals, and only the wealthy could afford to eat beef. From the 1770s, Robert Bakewell's experimentation with breeding, diet, and environment transformed cows into animals fit for the dinner table. Wealthy gentlemen, including the king, took a fashionably active interest in improving their livestock, and the craze for "improved" animals resulted in bloated beasts that were their owners' pride and joy.

Figure 118.2. Cow, to the left, with open cavity in the back of its body. H: 11.5", L: 18". Price E. *John Howard; www.antiquepottery.co.uk.*

Figure 118.1. Bull and cow, a pair, each with an open cavity in the body. L: 13.5" at the base. The largest cow models. Sizable openings at the back suggest they may have been placed in shop windows with a sign of sorts set in the hollow. Price G. *Dallas Auction Gallery.*

Figure 118.3. Cow, reverse of previous figure showing the large cavity. *John Howard; www. antiquepottery.co.uk.*

Figure 118.4. Cow, to the left; with spill vase. L~18". Like previous cows but there is no open cavity. Instead, a spill vase was added. Price E. *Elinor Penna.*

Figure 118.5. Cow, to the right; with spill vase. Impressed "WOOD & CALDWELL BURSLEM". L: ~12.5". Smaller than the previous cow models. Like the cows that follow but on a shorter base. A similarly marked horse pairs with this cow (fig. 125.6). Price D.

Figure 118.6. Cow, to the right; with spill vase. Attributed to Enoch Wood/Wood & Caldwell. L: 12.6". On a longer base than the previous cow. The large four-petalled flowers on the base are specific to this pot bank. Price D. *John Howard; www.antiquepottery.co.uk.*

Figure 118.7. Cow, to the right; with bocage. Attributed to Enoch Wood/ Wood & Caldwell. L: ~12.6". The four-petalled flowers strewn on the base support attribution. The acorns that are integral to the bocage are painted yellow and brown, as is typical of Enoch Wood bocages formed thus. Price D. *John Howard; www. antiquepottery.co.uk.*

Figure 118.8. Cow, reverse of previous figure. Unlike the fronts of the bocage leaves, the backs lack acorns. *John Howard; www.antiquepottery.co.uk.*

Figure 118.9. Cow, to the right; with bocage. Attributed to Enoch Wood/ Wood & Caldwell. L: ~12.6". Like the previous figure but painted differently and with less embellishment to the base. The left portion of the bocage is restored. Price C.

Figure 118.10. Bull, to the right and pawing the ground; with bocage. Attributed to Patriotic Group. H: 7.5". The bocage flowers are characteristic of the Patriotic Group. Pairs with the next cow. Price B. *Elinor Penna.*

Figure 118.11. Cow, to the left; with bocage. Attributed to Patriotic Group. H: 7.5". Pairs with the previous bull. Price B. *Elinor Penna.*

Figure 118.12. Cow, to the left; with bocage. Attributed to Patriotic Group. H: ~8". Price B. *Saffron Walden Museum.*

Figure 118.13. Cow, to the left, with raised rear leg; with bocage. Attributed to Patriotic Group. H: ~7". The bocage flowers are specific to the Group. The shredded clay in an arc along the front of the base is an unusual and attractive decorative touch. Price B. *Andrew Dando Antiques.*

Figure 118.14. Cow, to the left; with bocage. Attributed to Tunstall Group. H: ~7". The bocage flowers are specific to Tunstall. The large flowers on the base occur on other Tunstall figures. Price B. *John Howard; www.antiquepottery.co.uk.*

Figure 118.15. Cow, to the left, with rear leg raised to avoid a snake; with bocage. Attributed to Tunstall Group. H: 7.2". The bocage and its flowers support the attribution. Price A. *Barbara Gair; www.castle-antiques.com.*

Figure 118.16. Cows, a pair; with bocages. Attributed to Tunstall Group. H: 6.8". The characteristic bocage flowers match shards from the Tunstall site. Price C. *Eileen and Robert Carde.*

Figure 118.17. Cow to the right, cow to the left with rear leg raised to avoid a snake, a pair; with bocages. Attributed to Tunstall Group. H: 7.3". The cow to the right is as in the previous pair, but the cow to the left is modeled differently. Price C. *John Howard; www.antiquepottery.co.uk.*

Figure 118.18. Cow, to the right with rear leg raised to avoid a snake; with bocage. Attributed to Tunstall Group. H: ~7.3". Comparison with the previous Tunstall cows indicates that these models were made with or without a snake, so that assorted pairings are possible. Price B. *John Howard; www.antiquepottery.co.uk.*

Figure 118.20. Bull with tiger-striped coat, posed to the right as if being baited; with bocage. Attributed to Leaf Mat Group. H: 6". Price C. *John Howard; www.antiquepottery.co.uk.*

Figure 118.21. Bull, reverse of previous example. *John Howard; www.antiquepottery.co.uk.*

Figure 118.19. Cow, to the left with raised rear leg; with bocage. H: ~6.5". The flower stalks appear integral to the leaves and are painted to simulate flowers. Fluted impressions edging the base also occur on a cow-and-calf cow creamer (fig. 118.104). Price B.

Figure 118.22. Detail of the bocage and base of the previous bull. The flowers are arranged in pre-formed clusters of four and occur on at least one other Leaf Mat Group example, but the base is unusually elaborate for this pot bank. *John Howard; www.antiquepottery.co.uk.*

Figure 118.23. Bull, posed to the right as if being baited, with bocage and spill vase. H: 6.5". The large ten-petalled flower on the base occurs on the base of the previous Leaf Mat Group bull, but this alone does not support an attribution. Price B. *Dallas Auction Gallery.*

Figure 118.24. Cow, to the left with rear leg raised to avoid a snake; with bocage. H: ~6.5". Price A.

Figure 118.25. Cow, to the left with rear leg raised to avoid a snake; with bocage. H: 6.2". This and other similar figures reflect the myth that snakes suck milk from cows. Price B. *Brighton and Hove Museums.*

Figure 118.26. Cow, to the left with rear leg raised to avoid a snake; with bocage. Possibly made by Hall. H: ~6.5". The bocage with oak leaves and integral acorns painted red is suggestive of Hall. Price A.

Figure 118.27. Cow, to the left with rear leg raised to avoid a snake; with bocage. H: ~7". Pairs with a bull being baited (Vol. 2, fig. 83.17). Price B.

Figure 118.28. Cow, to the left with rear leg raised; with bocage. H: ~7". Price B.

Figure 118.29. Cow, to the left with rear leg raised to avoid a snake; with bocage. Attributed to "Sherratt." H: 7.5". This rainbow base is specific to "Sherratt." Price C. *John Howard; www.antiquepottery.co.uk.*

Figure 118.30. Cow, to the right, cow to the left with leg raised to avoid a snake, a pair; with bocages. Attributed to "Sherratt." H: 7.6". The combination of oak leaves and mayflowers comprising the bocage is exclusive to "Sherratt." Price D. *Elinor Penna.*

Figure 118.31. Cow, to the right; with bocage. Attributed to "Sherratt." H: 7.5". This waisted base occurs on other "Sherratt" figures. Price B. *Collection of Michael J. Smith.*

Figure 118.32. Cow to the right, cow to the left with leg raised to avoid a snake; a pair; with bocages. H: ~8". On the same bases as the previous cow but with characteristic "Sherratt" floral sprigs applied to each. Price B.

Figure 118.33. *CUP TOYDA*. Cow, to the right; with bocage. Attributed to "Sherratt." H: 8.2". The title was probably intended to read *CUP TODAY*. Milk was sold by the cup straight from the cow, "cup today" being the street vendor's call. Price B. *www.madelena.com.*

Figure 118.34. *CUP LADY.* Cow, to the left with rear leg raised to avoid a snake; with bocage. Attributed to "Sherratt." H: 9". *CUP LADY* refers to the name given the street vendor who accompanied the cow, selling milk by the cup. Price B.

Figure 118.35. Cow, to the left; with bocage. Attributed to Straw Flower Group. H: 6.3". Price B. *www.madelena.com.*

Figure 118.36. Cow, to the left. Attributed to Straw Flower Group. H: 6". Made without bocage. Price B. *John Howard; www.antiquepottery.co.uk.*

Figure 118.37. Cow, to the left. H: 6". Made without bocage. From the same molds as the previous cow but lacking features for attribution. Price A. *Barbara Gair; www.castle-antiques.com.*

Figure 118.38. Cow, to the right, with suckling calf; with bocage. Attributed to Dudson. H: ~5". Two bocage fronds are original, but the others are restored. Price A.

Figure 118.39. Cow, to the right, with suckling calf; with bocage. H: ~5". Price A.

Figure 118.40. Cow, to the right, with recumbent calf; with bocage. Attributed to Leather Leaf Group. H: 4.3". Several pot banks used these large bocage flowers, but the bocage leaves, the painting, and resemblances to the following figure confirm the attribution. Price A.

Figure 118.41. Cow, to the right, with recumbent calf; with bocage. Attributed to Leather Leaf Group. H: ~4.3". Like the previous cow, but here the bocage flowers are specific to the Group. Price A.

Figure 118.42. Cow, to the left, with recumbent calf; with bocage. Attributed to Leather Leaf Group. H: ~4.3". A subject pair to the previous cow. The very splotchy painting of the base is typical of the Group. Price A.

Figure 118.43. Cow with recumbent calf, to the right; with bocage. Impressed "SALT". H: 6". Price A.

Figure 118.44. Cow with recumbent calf, to the right; with bocage. H: 6". Like the previous Salt cow but unmarked. Other potters made figures just like Salt's, so this cow cannot be attributed. Companion model to the following cow. Price A.

Figure 118.45. Cow, to the left, with recumbent calf; with bocage. H: 6". Pairs with the previous cow and is in the style of Salt. Price A.

Figure 118.46. A pair of cows each with a recumbent calf; with bocages. H: 6". Unmarked with Salt-type bocages that cannot support attribution. Blue flowers are not documented on marked Salt figures. Price B. *John Howard; www.antiquepottery.co.uk.*

Figure 118.47. Cow with recumbent calf, to the right; with bocage. Attributed to Daisy Group. H: ~6". Price A.

Figure 118.48. Cow with recumbent calf, to the right; with detachable bocage. Attributed to Dale. H: ~5". The socket bocage is typical of Dale, as are the bocage leaves and flowers. Price B.

Figure 118.49. Cow, reverse of previous figure showing the bocage inserted in the socket.

Figure 118.50. Cow with recumbent calf, to the left; with detachable bocage. Attributed to Dale. H: ~5". The detachable bocage and the bocage leaves and flowers are typical of Dale. Price B. *Andrew Dando Antiques.*

Figure 118.51. Cow, to the left; with bocage. Probably made by Dale. H: ~5.5". These twelve-petalled bocage flowers occur only on figures attributable to Dale and on figures marked "TITTENSOR." Price A.

Figure 118.52. Cow with recumbent calf, to the left; with bocage. Probably made by Dale. H: ~5.5". The eight-petalled bocage flowers are of the type Dale used. Also, the extensive tooth-like marks on the base are typical of Dale. Price A.

Figure 118.53. Cow to the right; with bocage. H: 6.9". Price A.

Figure 118.54. Cow with recumbent calf, to the right; with bocage. Impressed "WALTON". H: 6.3". Price A.

Figure 118.55. A pair of cows, each with a recumbent calf and bocage. Impressed "WALTON". H: 6.3". Marked Walton cows are surprisingly uncommon. Price B. *John Howard; www. antiquepottery. co.uk.*

Figure 118.56. Cows, reverse of previous pair, both impressed "WALTON". *John Howard; www. antiquepottery. co.uk.*

Figure 118.57. Cow with two swans, to the left; with bocage. H: ~6.5". The only recorded example of this unusual grouping. The bocage flowers are uncommon, but there is no basis for attribution. Price B.

Figure 118.58. Cow to the right, with suckling calf. Attributed to Enoch Wood/Wood & Caldwell. H: 2.4". Bocage lost. Remarkable for the large flowers on the base that are specific to this manufactory. Price A. *Michael Goodacre.*

Figure 118.59. Cow, to the right, with suckling calf; with bocage. Attributed to Enoch Wood. H: 5". Like the previous and following figures. The bocage and base are typical of Enoch Wood. Price A.

Figure 118.60. Cow, to the right, with suckling calf; with bocage. Attributed to Enoch Wood. H: ~5". The bocage fronds (seven-leaflet fern fronds) and the base are as on the previous figure group, but the decoration is quite different. Like the following marked figure group. Price A.

Figure 118.61. A pair of cows, one with a suckling calf, the other with a recumbent calf; with bocages. Inscribed "E Wood & Son" (L); unmarked but attributed to Enoch Wood (R). H: ~5". Price A.

Figure 118.62. The base of the previous figure of a cow with suckling calf with the "E Wood & Son" inscription. Comparing this inscription to Enoch Wood's handwriting suggests it is in his own hand. This is the only figure known to be marked in this way.

Figure 118.63. Cow, to the right, with suckling calf; with bocage. Attributed to Enoch Wood. H: 5.2". The bocage fronds (one leaflet upon four) differ from the fern fronds on previous Enoch Wood examples, but they are also typical of Enoch Wood. Price A.

Figure 118.64. Cow with recumbent calf, to the left; with bocage. Attributed to Enoch Wood. H: ~5". A companion to the previous figure, having the same base and bocage fronds but different bocage flowers. Price A.

Figure 118.65. Cow, to the right, with suckling calf; with bocage. Attributed to Enoch Wood. H: 5". Price A. *Nicholas Frost Antiques.*

Figure 118.66. Cow, to the right, with recumbent calf; with bocage. H: 5.7". Companion to the following figure. Price A. *Andrew Dando Antiques.*

Figure 118.67. Cow with recumbent calf, to the left; with bocage. H: ~5.7". Companion to the preceding figure. Both have bocage fronds with one leaflet atop three others, a form used by several potters. Price A.

Figure 118.68. Cow with recumbent calf, to the left; with bocage. H: ~5.8". From the same molds as the previous cow, but with hawthorn leaves for the bocage fronds. This figure and the previous two cows may have come from the same pot bank. Price A.

Figure 118.69. Cow with recumbent calf, to the left; with bocage. Attributed to Patriotic Group. H: ~5.7". Price A.

Figure 118.70. Cow, to the right, with recumbent calf; with bocage. Attributed to Patriotic Group. H: ~5.7". The flowers on the bocage support the attribution. Price A.

Figure 118.71. Cow with recumbent calf, to the right; with bocage. Attributed to Patriotic Group. H: ~6". This pot bank also used this base for other figures. Price A.

Figure 118.72. Cow, to the right, with recumbent calf; with bocage. H: ~6". Unusual, large bocage leaves with the pink carnations favored by many pot banks. Price A.

Figure 118.73. Cow, to the left; with bocage. H: ~5". Price A.

Figure 118.74. Cow, to the right, with recumbent calf; with bocage. H: ~5". Price A.

Figure 118.75. Cow, to the left, with recumbent calf; with bocage. H: ~5". Price A.

Figure 118.76. Cow, to the right; with bocage. Attributed to "Sherratt." H: ~4.3". The floral sprigs applied to the base are akin to signatures on "Sherratt" figures. "Sherratt" sometimes used this turquoise palette. Companion subject to the following cow. Price A.

Figure 118.77. Cow, to the left; with bocage. Attributed to "Sherratt." H: ~4.3". A companion subject to the preceding cow but with a different bocage that is also consistent with a "Sherratt" attribution. Price A.

Figure 118.78. Bull, to the right, cow with calf to the left, both with bocages, an assembled pair. Attributed to "Sherratt." H: ~4". The bocages support the attribution. The mottled painting of the tree trunks occurs on other "Sherratt" figures. Price B.

Figure 118.79. Bull, to the right, with recumbent calf. Attributed to "Sherratt." H: ~4.5". This base occurs on other small "Sherratt" figures, and this bull model is exclusive to "Sherratt." Bocage restored. Price A.

Figure 118.80. Recumbent cow, to the right; with bocage. H: ~3.5". These three-leaflet bocage fronds occur on an unclassified array of fine figures. Price A.

Figure 118.83. Recumbent cow, to the right; with bocage. Probably made by Enoch Wood. H: ~3.5". The bocage and base are typical of Enoch Wood. Companion to the following cow. Price A.

Figure 118.81. Recumbent cow, to the left; with bocage. H: ~3.5". Price A.

Figure 118.82. Recumbent cow, to the left; with bocage. Probably attributable to Patriotic Group. H: ~4". The bocage (with some restoration) is consistent with the attribution. Price A.

Figure 118.84. Bocage on the previous cow. The fronds comprise one leaflet atop three in a typical Enoch Wood manner.

Figure 118.85. Recumbent cow, to the left; with bocage. Probably made by Enoch Wood. H: 3.2". The bocage has one leaflet atop three, as on the previous companion cow. Price A. *Michael Goodacre.*

Figure 118.86. Small pair of recumbent cows; with bocages. H: 2.2". Price A.

Figure 118.87. Small pair of recumbent cows; with bocages. Impressed "SALT". H: 2.1". The cows are from the same molds as the previous pair, but the bocages are different. Salt made deer and sheep in the same style (figs. 119.173, 131.177). Price A.

Figure 118.88. Small recumbent cow; with bocage. Probably attributable to Patriotic Group. H: 3". The bocage comprises a holly leaf with the back unpainted. This leaf is otherwise found only on Patriotic Group figures, always paired back-to-back with another leaf, and always with the berries painted pink/red. Price A. *John B. Watson.*

Figure 118.89. Two cows, each with a recumbent calf and bocage, each flanking a spill vase. L: 10". A finely executed example on a petite scale. Similarly styled spill vases flanked by deer or sheep are significantly larger, measuring about 15" across. Price D.

Figure 118.90. Two cows, each with a recumbent calf and bocage, each flanking a spill vase. L: 10". Like the previous example but in a less variegated palette. Much rarer than the larger but conceptually similar groups with deer. Price D.

Figure 118.91. Two cows and a calf, with a spill vase. H: ~7.5". Attributed to "Sherratt." Known from only this example. This base is exclusive to "Sherratt," and some other "Sherratt" spill vases are painted in the same manner. Price C.

Figure 118.92. Bull before a spill vase. H: ~7". Price B. *John Howard; www.antiquepottery.co.uk.*

Figure 118.93. Two cows before a spill vase, with an owl and squirrel on the vase. H: 8.1". Price B. *Andrew Dando Antiques.*

Figure 118.94. Two cows with calves and sheep, with a spill vase. Probably attributable to Patriotic Group. H: 6.9". This base otherwise occurs only on examples confidently attributed to the Patriotic Group. Price *C. W. W. Warner Antiques.*

Figure 118.95. A pair of cows, each before a spill vase. Attributed to Dale. H: 6.6"(L), 6.2"(R). Part of a three-piece garniture (Vol.1, fig. 27.166). The floral sprigs on the bases only occur on Dale figures. Price B. *Elinor Penna.*

Figure 118.96. Reverse of the previous cow on the right. A similar pattern of curves and hollows occurs on the bocage tree trunks of some marked Dale figures. The bright apple-green painting is typical of Dale. *Elinor Penna.*

Figure 118.97. Cow with recumbent calf, to the right; with spill vase. Attributed to Patriotic Group. H: 5". Sprigs characteristic of the Patriotic Group are on the base. Price A. *Barbara Gair; www.castle-antiques.com.*

Figure 118.98. Cow, to the right, with bocage and spill vase. H: ~6". Enoch Wood favored yellow acorns on his oak leaf bocages, but nothing else about this group suggests that attribution. Price A.

Figure 118.99. Cow with recumbent calf, to the right, with bocage and spill vase. Marked "WALTON". H: ~7.2". Walton made similarly styled sheep. A companion subject to the following figure. Price A.

Figure 118.100. Cow, to the left, with recumbent calf, with bocage and spill vase. Marked "WALTON". A companion subject to the previous figure. Both are uncommon. Price A.

Figure 118.101. Cow with recumbent calf, to the left; with spill vase. Marked "WALTON". H: ~6.5". Price A.

Figure 118.102. Cow, to the right; with spill vase. H: 3.9". Probably made by the Scottish east coast potteries. Price A. *Andrew Dando Antiques.*

Figure 118.103. Cow creamer. L: 13.5". This is an extraordinarily large creamer. Early creamers are more usually decorated in under-glaze colors, a cheaper technique better suited for useful wares. Price C. *Jonathan Horne.*

Figure 118.104. Cow creamer with calf. H: ~6". Calves are not usually present on cow creamers. Decorated with both under-glaze and enamel colors. Price C. *John Howard; www.antiquepottery.co.uk.*

Figure 118.105. Cow creamer. L: 6.5". By around 1830, enamel painting had become more affordable, and an increasing number of cow creamers were painted in this manner. Price A. *Martyn Edgell Antiques Ltd.*

Figure 118.106. Cow creamer. L: 7.4". Probably made at the Cambrian Pottery in Wales. Welsh cow creamers are distinguished by the cow's protruding breastbones. Price A. *William Brook.*

Figure 118.107. Cow creamer. L: 6.5". Concerns about hygiene in the Victorian era led to the demise of cow creamers. Price A. *www.madelena.com.*

119. Deer

By the eighteenth century, deer hunting had waned in popularity because deer populations had shriveled and there were fewer open sweeps of land necessary for the chase. Although a few packs carried on the ancient tradition of deer hunting, hunts had become staged exercises, and a mature stag was invariably "uncarted" for the occasion. Such events had lost much of the thrill, so deer were increasingly regarded as appropriate adornments for gentlemen's parks rather than quarry for slaughter. Figures of deer were refined decoration for elegant homes, and an astounding array was made. Today, many have suffered almost inevitable damage to their antlers. While restored antlers are common, a fine pair of antlers in original condition enhances the appearance and value of earthenware deer.

Figure 119.1. Deer hunted by three dogs. Attributed to Enoch Wood/Wood & Caldwell. H: 6.7". The flowers on the base are characteristic of this manufactory. Known only from this example. Price E. *Bonhams.*

Figure 119.2. Deer and stag each with a bocage, along with a piper and two sheep, all with a spill vase. H: 9.7", L: 15". Each bocage frond has two leaflets atop three others. Probably from the same pot bank as the following two examples. Price D. *John Howard; www.antiquepottery.co.uk.*

Figure 119.3. Deer and stag each with bocage, along with a piper and two sheep, all with a spill vase. H: 10.3", L: 15". The bocage comprises small leaflets, arranged in perhaps twos or threes. The flowers match those on the following example from the same pot bank. Price D. © *Fitzwilliam Museum, Cambridge.*

Figure 119.4. Deer and stag each with bocage, along with a piper, dog, and two sheep, all with a spill vase. L: ~15". Closely similar to the previous example, but here each unusual bocage frond comprises three large leaflets. Price D.

Figure 119.5. Deer and stag each with bocage, along with a sheep, all with a spill vase. Attributed to Enoch Wood. L ~15". The bocages and flowers on the base support the attribution. The deer are made separately from the base and can be removed. This pair is not original to this base. See figure 131.222 for a similar vase with sheep. Price B.

Figure 119.6. Stag, to the left; with bocage. H: 13.4". The impressive antlers on this stag are original. Price B.

Figure 119.7. Stag, to the left; with bocage. H: 9". A whole bocage frond and some partial fronds are applied to the unusual base. Price B. *Nick Burton.*

Figure 119.8. Stag, reverse of previous figure. Each bocage frond comprises five leaflets. *Nick Burton.*

Figure 119.9. Pair of deer, each with bocage. H: ~6.2". The bocages are in the Salt style, but no similar marked Salt figures are recorded. Salt's recumbent deer occur without antlers. Like these, they show the painter's finger prints on each coat spot. Price B.

Figure 119.10. Stag, to the left; with bocage. H: ~6.2". Perhaps a companion subject to the following doe. Price A.

Figure 119.11. Doe, to the right; with bocage. H: ~6.5". As on the previous figure, the Salt-style bocage has pink and blue carnations. Blue carnations are not recorded on marked Salt figures. Price A. *Andrew Dando Antiques.*

Figure 119.12. Deer, to the left; with bocage. H: ~5.4". Price A.

Figure 119.13. Deer, to the left; with bocage. H: ~5". Price A.

Figure 119.14. Deer, to the right; with bocage. H: ~5.7". The bocage flowers are carnations. Price A.

Figure 119.15. Pair of deer; with bocages. H: ~5.8". The deer facing right has six-petalled bocage flowers. The deer facing left has carnations on the bocage, like the deer in figure 119.14. Price B.

Figure 119.16. Deer, to the right; with bocage. H: ~6.5". Price A.

Figure 119.17. Deer, to the right; with bocage. H: ~6.5". Floral sprigs are integral to the base. Price A.

Figure 119.18. Detail of the previous figure's unusual base.

Figure 119.19. Deer, to the right; with bocage. Probably attributable to Straw Flower Group. H: ~5.4". Each tiny bocage flower has five cleft petals, as occur on Straw Flower Group figures. Price A.

Figure 119.20. Deer, to the right, with bocage: H: ~6.3". Unusual bocage leaves, and each tiny bocage flower has ten petals. Price A.

Figure 119.21. Pair of deer; with bocages. Attributed to Daisy Group. H: ~7" max. Price B.

Figure 119.22. Pair of deer; with bocages. Attributed to Starred Anthemion Group. H: 6"(L), 6.2"(R). Price A. *Elinor Penna.*

Figure 119.23. Stag, to the left; with bocage. Attributed to Big Blossom Group. H: ~5.7". Price A.

119.24. Deer, to the right; with bocage. Attributed to Big Blossom Group. H: ~5.7". Bocage restored. The flowers on the base are original and support the attribution. Price A.

Figure 119.25. Deer, to the left; with bocage. Attributed to Tunstall Group. H: ~5.5". The bocage flowers are specific to Tunstall. Price A.

Figure 119.26. Deer, to the left; with bocage. Attributed to Tunstall Group. H: ~5.5". The base is like that of the following stag. Price A.

Figure 119.27. Stag, to the left; with bocage. Attributed to Tunstall Group. H: ~5.8". On the same base as the previous Tunstall deer, but the figure is different. Price A.

Figure 119.28. Stag, to the right; with bocage. Attributed to Patriotic Group. H: ~6". The large bocage leaves are unusual and atypical, but both the base and flowers are specific to Patriotic Group. Companion subject to the following doe. Price A.

Figure 119.29. Doe, to the left; with bocage. Attributed to Patriotic Group. H: ~6". A companion subject to the previous stag and has a typical Patriotic Group bocage and base. Price A.

Figure 119.30. A pair of deer, each with bocage. Attributed to Patriotic Group. H: ~6". The deer are from the same molds as the two preceding Patriotic Group figures. Price B.

Figure 119.31. Stag, to the right; with bocage. Attributed to Patriotic Group. H: 6.2". Like the stag in the previous pair but with different bocage flowers and painting. Price B. *Collection of Susan and Richard Cann.*

Figure 119.32. Stag, reverse of previous figure. These bocage fronds (one leaflet atop five others) occur most commonly on Patriotic Group figures. *Collection of Susan and Richard Cann.*

Figure 119.33. Stag, to the right; with bocage. Attributed to Patriotic Group. H: ~6.1". Pairs with the following doe. Price A.

Figure 119.34. Doe, to the left; with bocage. Attributed to Patriotic Group. H: ~5.9". Pairs with the previous stag and, like it, has characteristic Patriotic Group bocage flowers. Price A.

Figure 119.35. Doe, to the right; with bocage. Attributed to Patriotic Group. H: 7". This doe is larger than previous Patriotic Group examples. The bocage is like that on figure 119.31, from the same pot bank. Price A. *Michael Goodacre.*

Figure 119.36. Stag, to the left; with bocage. Attributed to Patriotic Group. H: ~7.4". Price A.

Figure 119.37. Deer, to the right; with bocage. Attributed to Dale. H: ~6". The characteristic floral sprigs on the base and the twelve-petalled bocage flowers support the attribution. Price A.

Figure 119.38. An assembled pair of deer; with bocages. Possibly made by Dale. H: ~6.5" max. The doe is from the same molds as the previous doe. The bocage flowers are consistent with a Dale attribution. Price A.

Figure 119.39. Doe, to the right; with bocage. Attributed to Dudson. H: ~6.4". Price A.

Figure 119.40. A pair of deer; with bocages. Attributed to Dudson. H: 7.3" max. The doe is like the previous doe, but the base is different. Price A. *K. Gomersall.*

Figure 119.41. Deer, to the right; with bocage. Attributed to Dudson. H: ~6.5". Price A.

Figure 119.42. Deer, to the left; with bocage. H: ~6.5". Price A.

Figure 119.43. Deer, to the left; with bocage. H: ~6.5. An unusual asterisk is deeply impressed beneath the base. The base and clusters of small pointed five-petalled bocage flowers are as on the previous figure. These bocage flowers occur on an array of unclassified figures with common features. Price A.

Figure 119.44. Doe, to the right; with bocage. Attributed to Hall. H: ~5.5". The flowers are painted like those on marked Hall figures. The unusual arched support for the bocage is also on the following doe attributed to Hall. Price A.

Figure 119.45. A pair of deer; with bocages. Attributed to Hall. H: ~5.5" max. The doe, like the previous doe, has an unusual arched bocage support. The bocage flowers and the painting style (also seen on recumbent deer) are associated with Hall. Price A.

Figure 119.46. A pair of deer; with bocages. Attributed to Hall. H: ~5.5" max. The star-like flowers on the stag's bocage link to Hall. Unlike the previous pair, both animals have arched bocage supports. Restoration to doe's bocage. Price A.

Figure 119.47. Doe, to the right; with bocage. Attributed to Enoch Wood. H: 7.1". The bocage fronds (seven-leaflet fern fronds) and base are typical of Enoch Wood. The same model as the following Enoch Wood doe. Price A. *www.madelena.com.*

Figure 119.48. Pair of deer; with bocages. Attributed to Enoch Wood. H: 6"(L), 8"(R). The large flowers on the base of the doe are characteristic of this manufactory. Price A. *Barbara Gair; www.castle-antiques.com.*

Figure 119.49. Pair of deer, previous pair. The typical Enoch Wood bocage fronds have one leaflet atop four others. A workman's initials, "NN", are scratched into the clay of the stag's base. *Barbara Gair; www.castle-antiques.com.*

Figure 119.50. Deer, to the right; with bocage. Attributed to Leather Leaf Group. H: ~6.3". The bocage is restored, but the flowers and leaves on the base confirm the attribution. Price A.

Figure 119.51. Doe, to the right; with bocage. Attributed to "Sherratt." H: ~7.1". The largest "Sherratt" deer are recorded only on such oval bases. The mottled painting on the bocage trunk is seen on other "Sherratt" figures. Price B.

Figure 119.52. Doe, to the right; with bocage. Attributed to "Sherratt." H: ~7.1". Like the previous doe but painted differently. Painters frequently used their fingers to make the spots in deer coats, thus leaving their prints on the spots, but "Sherratt" spots are never done in this way. Price B.

Figure 119.53. Stag, to the left; with bocage. Attributed to "Sherratt." H: 7.9". A companion to previous large "Sherratt" does. Note the luster decoration. Price B.

Figure 119.54. Stag, to the left; with bocage. Attributed to "Sherratt." H: 6". This stag is significantly smaller than previous "Sherratt" examples. Price A.

Figure 119.55. Stag, to the left; with bocage. Attributed to "Sherratt." H: 6". Like the previous stag but with different bocage flowers. Price A.

Figure 119.56. Doe with fawn, to the right; stag to the left. A pair with bocages. Attributed to "Sherratt." H: 6.1". This unusual pair differs from previous and following "Sherratt" deer of the same scale. Price B. *Elinor Penna.*

Figure 119.57. Doe with fawn to the right; stag with fawn to the left. A pair; with bocages. Attributed to "Sherratt." H: 5.8" max. This stag differs from previous "Sherratt" stags. Price B.

Figure 119.58. Doe with fawn to the right; stag with fawn to the left. A pair; with bocages. Attributed to "Sherratt." H: ~6" max. Like the previous pair but with different "Sherratt" bocages. These models are more common than the small "Sherratt" pair in figure 119.56. Price B.

Figure 119.59. Stag with fawn, to the left; with bocage. Attributed to "Sherratt." H: ~6". Like the previous stag but with large spots. Price A.

Figure 119.60. Doe with fawn to the right; with bocage. Attributed to "Sherratt." H: ~5.7". "Sherratt" deer are quirkier in appearance than those from other pot banks and are sometimes painted in this pink shade. Price A.

Figure 119.61. Doe with fawn to the right; with bocage. Attributed to "Sherratt." H: ~5.7". The base is formed like previous "Sherratt" bases, but here characteristic "Sherratt" sprigs are applied to it. The bocage differs from those on the previous small "Sherratt" deer. Price A.

Figure 119.62. Doe with fawn to the right; with bocage. Attributed to "Sherratt." H: ~5.5". The fawn is much larger than the fawn on the previous "Sherratt" examples. The base and bocage are also different, but they are typical of "Sherratt." Price A.

Figure 119.63. Stag, to the left; with bocage. H: ~6." Price A.

Figure 119.64. Stag, to the right; with bocage. H: ~8". This bocage is not otherwise recorded. Price B.

Figure 119.65. Stag, to the left; with bocage. H: ~6". The bocage fronds each comprise three hawthorn leaves. Price A. *John Howard; www. antiquepottery.co.uk.*

Figure 119.66. Stag, to the left; with bocage. H: ~7". A very unusual example. Price B. *Jonathan Horne.*

Figure 119.67. Deer, to the right; with bocage. H: ~5.8". Price A.

Figure 119.68. Stag, to the left; with bocage. H: 6". Price A.

Figure 119.69. A pair of deer; with bocages. H: ~6.5" max. The bocages are restored. Price A.

Figure 119.70. Deer, to the right; with bocage. H: ~7". Price A.

Figure 119.71. A pair of deer; with bocages. H: ~6.2" max. The stag's bocage and the right section of the doe's bocage are restored. Price A.

Figure 119.72. Doe with fawn, to the right; with spill vase. H: 6". Decorated with enamel and possibly under-glaze colors. Perhaps made by one of the northeast pot banks. Companion to the following spill vase. Price A. *The William Herbert and Nancy Hunt Collection.*

Figure 119.73. Deer, to the left; with spill vase. H: 6". Decorated with enamel and possibly under-glaze colors. Perhaps made by one of the northeast pot banks and is a companion to the previous example. Price A. *Robert Hawker.*

Figure 119.74. Deer, to the right; with spill vase. H: 6". The colors suggest manufacture by one of the Scottish pot banks or a pot bank in the northeast of England. Price A. *W. W. Warner Antiques.*

Figure 119.75. A pair of deer, each with spill vase. H: 5.5". Painted in colors suggesting manufacture by a Scottish pot bank or a pot bank in the northeast of England. Price B. *W. W. Warner Antiques.*

Figure 119.76. A stag, doe, and fawn, with birds and a spill vase. H: 8.4". Possibly made by one of the Scottish pot banks or a pot bank in the northeast of England. Price B. *Bardith Ltd.*

Figure 119.77. Large recumbent stag, to the left. H: 8.5", L: 11.5". This model when found decorated in colored glazes is usually associated with Ralph Wood. Price B. *The William Herbert and Nancy Hunt Collection.*

Figure 119.78. Large recumbent deer, to the right. H: 7.5", L: 11". Price B. *The William Herbert and Nancy Hunt Collection.*

Figure 119.79. A pair of recumbent deer, each with a squirrel and a spill vase. H: 5"; L: 5.5". Other spill vase groups (figs. 123.7, 126.136–137, 131.94–95, and Vol. 4, fig. 197.79) with vases of the same form appear to be from the same pot bank. Price B. *Collection of Michael J. Smith.*

Figure 119.81. Recumbent deer, to the right; with bocage. Possibly made by Ralph Wood. H: ~5.8". The bocage and the rainbow-like decoration of the base are typical of Ralph Wood. Price A.

Figure 119.80. A pair of recumbent deer, each with a squirrel and a spill vase. H: 4.8"; L: 3.8". In the same style as the previous pair, and, again only one animal has spots. Price B. *Collection of Michael J. Smith.*

Figure 119.82. Recumbent doe, to the right. H: 5.5". Made without bocage. Pairs with the following stag. Price B, pair. *Collection of Susan and Richard Cann.*

Figure 119.83. Recumbent stag, to the left. H: 7". Made without bocage. Pairs with the previous doe. Price B, pair. *Collection of Susan and Richard Cann.*

Figure 119.84. Recumbent doe, to the right. H: 3.8", L: 4.4". Made without a bocage. Price A.

Figure 119.85. A pair of recumbent deer. Made without bocages. H: 7.2" max. Price B. *Andrew Dando Antiques.*

Figure 119.86. Recumbent deer, to the right. Possibly made by the Swinton Pottery. L: 7". Holes atop the head accommodate metal antlers. A deer of this form and on this base is recorded impressed "BRAMELD/5" (the mark of the Bramelds at the Swinton Pottery). Price B. *Collection of Michael J. Smith.*

Figure 119.87. Recumbent deer, to the right. Possibly made by the Swinton Pottery. L: 7". Like the previous deer and also with holes for antlers. Price B. *John Howard; www.antiquepottery.co.uk.*

Figure 119.88. Recumbent deer, to the right. Possibly made by the Swinton Pottery. L: 7.5". Holes atop the head accommodate antlers. The deer is like the previous two deer, but the base differs. Price B. *John Howard; www.antiquepottery.co.uk.*

Figure 119.89. An assembled pair of recumbent deer; with bocages. Attributed to "Sherratt." H: ~4.5" max. The bocages support the attribution. Price A.

Figure 119.90. Recumbent doe with fawn, to the right; with bocage. Attributed to "Sherratt." H: ~4.8". Most "Sherratt" recumbent deer are in the same style as the small standing "Sherratt" deer in figures 119.54–62. Price A.

Figure 119.91. Recumbent doe with fawn, to the right; with bocage. Attributed to "Sherratt." H: ~4.8". Like the previous doe but with a different bocage. "Sherratt" often thoughtfully placed three small flowers on the front of bases such as this. Price A.

Figure 119.92. Recumbent doe, to the right; with bocage. Attributed to "Sherratt." H: ~4". The base and bocage are typical of "Sherratt." Price A.

Figure 119.93. Recumbent doe, to the right; with bocage. Attributed to Tunstall Group. H: ~5.5". The flowers are specific to the Group. Price A.

Figure 119.94. Recumbent stag, to the right; with bocage. Attributed to Tunstall Group. H: ~4.4". Price A.

Figure 119.95. Recumbent deer, to the right; with bocage. Attributed to Tunstall Group. H: 4.5". Price A. *Collection of Susan and Richard Cann.*

Figure 119.96. A pair of recumbent deer; with bocages. Attributed to Tunstall Group. H: ~4.5". Price A.

Figure 119.97. Recumbent stag, to the left. Attributed to Tunstall Group. H: ~5.5". The bocage differs from those on the previous "Tunstall" pair. Price A.

Figure 119.98. Recumbent doe, to the right; with bocage. Attributed to Patriotic Group. H: ~3.5". The bocage leaves are unusual, but the bocage flower is specific to the Patriotic Group. The doe is from the same molds as the following doe. Price A.

Figure 119.99. A pair of recumbent deer; with bocages. Attributed to Patriotic Group. H: ~4" max. Flowers painted yellow and these bocage leaves (also on the bocage of the following figure) are uncommon on Patriotic Group figures. Price A.

Figure 119.100. Recumbent stag, to the left. Attributed to Patriotic Group. H: ~3.8". Like the previous stag, but the bocage flower is painted more typically. Price A.

Figure 119.101. Recumbent doe, to the right; with bocage. Attributed to Dudson. H: ~6.5". Pairs with the following stag. Price A. © *National Trust/Geoff Lowsley; www.nationaltrust.org.uk.*

Figure 119.102. Recumbent stag, to the left; with bocage. Attributed to Dudson. H: ~7". Pairs with the previous doe. Price A. © *National Trust/Geoff Lowsley; www.nationaltrust.org.uk.*

Figure 119.103. Recumbent stag, to the left; with spill vase and bocage. Possibly made by Patriotic Group. H: ~6.2". The bocage (despite some restoration) suggests the attribution. Price A.

Figure 119.104. Recumbent stag, to the left. Attributed to Patriotic Group. H: 7.2". The holly bocage is specific to the Group. Price A.

Figure 119.105. Recumbent stag, to the left. Probably attributable to Patriotic Group. H: ~7". The bocage has one leaflet atop five. Price A.

Figure 119.106. Recumbent deer, to the right. Attributed to Patriotic Group. H: ~4". The bocage flowers are specific to this Group. Price A.

Figure 119.107. Recumbent deer, to the left. Attributed to Patriotic Group. H: ~4". Price A.

Figure 119.108. A pair of recumbent deer; with bocages. Attributed to Patriotic Group. H: 5.2"(L), 4.8"(R). Price B.

Figure 119.109. Two recumbent deer, to the left; with bocages. H: 4.8"(L), 5.3"(R). Attributed to Patriotic Group (L) and impressed "SALT" (R). These two deer differ only in the formation of the bocages and in the sprigs on the bases. Price A each.

Figure 119.110. Pair of recumbent deer; with bocages. Marked "SALT". H: 5.3". In original condition, and both made without antlers. The spots on the coat were made by removing wet paint with the finger, leaving a fingerprint on each. Price B.

Figure 119.111. Pair of recumbent deer, reverse of previous pair, showing the "SALT" marks.

Figure 119.112. Pair of recumbent deer; with bocages. H: ~6.5" max. The bocages are very like those on the previous Salt pair, but the deer are quite different and probably originated from another pot bank. The antlers are restored. Price B.

Figure 119.113. Recumbent doe, to the left; with bocage. H: ~5". Like the previous stag but without antlers. Price A.

Figure 119.114. Recumbent deer, to the left; with bocage. Impressed "SALT". H: ~5". This figure is unique in that it has the Salt mark in small letters on a parallelogram-shaped plaque. Larger than previous Salt deer and on an atypical base. The companion to this deer is not recorded. Price A.

Figure 119.115. Recumbent doe, to the right; with bocage. H: ~4". A companion to the following stag. Price A.

Figure 119.116. Recumbent stag, to the left; with bocage. H: ~4.3". A companion to the previous doe. Price A.

Figure 119.117. Recumbent doe, to the right; with bocage. H: ~4.5". Like the doe in figure 119.115, but the base and bocage flowers are painted differently. Price A.

Figure 119.118. Recumbent doe, to the right; with bocage. H: ~4.5". Like the preceding doe, but the bocage flowers are not carnations and instead have ten small petals. Pairs with the following stag. Price A.

Figure 119.119. Recumbent stag, to the left; with bocage. H: ~4.6". Pairs with the previous doe and, like it, has ten-petalled bocage flowers. Price A.

Figure 119.120. Recumbent deer, to the left; with bocage. H: 5.9". Essentially of the same scale as the marked Salt pair in figure 119.110, but the bocage is taller. Price A.

Figure 119.121. Recumbent stag, to the left; with bocage. H: 4.3". As sometimes happens with small stags, the vulnerable antlers were potted as one thick structure. Price A.

Figure 119.122. A pair of recumbent deer; with bocages. H: ~5". The bocage fronds are of a type normally found on small figures with bocage sprigs fanning out to either side. Flower stalks are painted to simulate flowers. Price A.

Figure 119.123. An assembled pair of recumbent deer; with bocages. Attributed to Dudson. H: ~5". Both figures have bases and bocages (one leaflet atop seven leaflets) used by Dudson. Price A.

Figure 119.124. A pair of recumbent deer; with bocages. Attributed to Dudson. H: ~5". Each bocage frond has four rather asymmetrically arranged leaves. Price B.

Figure 119.125. Recumbent doe, to the left; with bocage. Attributed to Dudson. H: ~5". The bocage (four asymmetrical leaves in each frond) supports the attribution. Price A

Figure 119.126. Recumbent stag, to the right; with bocage. Attributed to Dudson. H: ~5". The unusual white antlers are original. Price A. *Andrew Dando Antiques.*

Figure 119.127. Recumbent stag, to the right; with bocage. Possibly made by Dudson. H: ~5". The bocage (with loss and restoration) is very suggestive of Dudson. Price A.

Figure 119.128. Recumbent doe, to the left; with bocage. H: 5". Flower stalks on the bocage leaves are painted green. Price A. *Collection of Michael J. Smith.*

Figure 119.129. Recumbent deer, to the right; with bocage. Attributed to Big Blossom Group. H: 5.5". Price A.

Figure 119.130. Recumbent stag, to the left; with bocage. Attributed to Big Blossom Group. H: ~4". Price A.

Figure 119.131. Recumbent deer, to the right; with bocage. Attributed to Leaf Mat Group. H: ~3.9". Price A.

Figure 119.132. A pair of recumbent deer; with bocages. Attributed to Starred Anthemion Group. H: ~5.7" max. Price B.

Figure 119.133. Recumbent doe, to the right; with bocage. Attributed to Starred Anthemion Group. H: ~6". With the same distinctive bocage as the previous pair, but this is a larger model. A companion stag is recorded. Price A.

Figure 119.134. Recumbent stag, to the right; with bocage. Probably attributable to Box Title Group. H: ~4.4". The painting of the carnations and the stalky bocage are typical of the Group. Slightly larger than the Box Title stags in figures 119.136–137 and facing the other way. Price A.

Figure 119.135. Recumbent doe, to the right; with bocage. Attributed to Box Title Group. H: 4". Pairs with the following stag. Price A. *www.madelena.com.*

Figure 119.136. Recumbent stag, to the left; with bocage. Attributed to Box Title Group. H: ~4". Pairs with the previous doe. The painting of the carnations and other features support attribution. Price A.

Figure 119.137. A pair of recumbent deer; with bocages. Attributed to Box Title Group. H: 4". Like the previous small Box Title deer, these figures have unusual tooling on the bocage trunks. Price A. *Andrew Dando Antiques.*

Figure 119.138. Two recumbent stags, both to the right; with bocages. Attributed to Hall (L), probably made by Hall (R). H: ~4". The stag on the left has the distinctive star-like bocage flowers associated with Hall. Both stags are painted in the same style as standing deer attributed to Hall. Price A.

Figure 119.139. Recumbent deer, to the right; with bocage. Probably made by Hall. H: ~3". Painted in the same style as standing deer by Hall. The bocage is consistent with a Hall attribution. Price A

Figure 119.140. Recumbent stag, to the right; with bocage. Probably made by Hall. H: ~4.8". This bocage is very suggestive of Hall. Price A.

Figure 119.141. A pair of recumbent deer; with bocages. Attributed to Blue Group. H: ~5.3" max. The bocage leaves and flowers, rather than the blue bases, establish the attribution. Price A.

Figure 119.142. Recumbent stag, to the left; with bocage. Impressed "WALTON". H: 3.6". The only marked Walton deer model, and the only marked Walton figure with this bocage. The leaves are not the same as the anthemion leaves Walton sometimes used. Price A.

119.143. Recumbent stag, to the right; with bocage. Possibly made by Enoch Wood. H: ~4". The bocage fronds have one leaflet atop three others. Price A.

Figure 119.144. Recumbent stag, to the right; with bocage. Attributed to Dudson. H: ~3.8". Price A.

Figure 119.145. Recumbent stag, to the right; with bocage. H: ~3.8". The hawthorn bocage leaves are not specific to any one pot bank. Price A.

Figure 119.146. Recumbent deer, to the right; with bocage. H: ~3.2". The bocage fronds comprise hawthorn leaves. Price A.

Figure 119.147. Recumbent stag, to the right; with bocage. H: ~3.8". Each bocage frond has three leaflets. Probably from the same pot bank as the following doe. Price A.

Figure 119.148. Recumbent doe, to the right; with bocage. H: 3.5". Each bocage frond has three leaflets. Probably from the same pot bank as the previous stag. Price A. *www.madelena.com.*

Figure 119.149. Recumbent deer, to the right. Attributed to Dudson. H: ~6". Bocage fronds (with one leaflet asymmetrically atop three) are consistent with the attribution. Price A.

Figure 119.150. Recumbent stag, to the left. Attributed to Dudson. H: ~7.2". The bocage supports the attribution. The base is molded to match the base in the previous example. Price A.

Figure 119.151. Recumbent doe, to the right. Possibly made by Enoch Wood. H: ~6". The bocage fronds each comprise seven tiny fern leaflets and are suggestive of the attribution. Price A.

Figure 119.152. Recumbent stag, to the left. Possibly made by Enoch Wood. H: ~6". Bocage fronds (each comprising seven tiny fern leaflets) are consistent with attribution, but they are not specific to Enoch Wood. Price A.

Figure 119.153. Recumbent stag, to the right; with bocage. Attributed to Dale. H: ~5.3". The floral sprig on the center of the bocage (a big five-petalled flower with three leaves, painted predominantly green) is specific to Dale. Price A.

Figure 119.154. Recumbent deer, to the right; with bocage. H: 5.6". In the style of John Walton but probably made by some other pot bank. Price A.

Figure 119.155. Recumbent deer, to the right; with bocage. H: ~5.6". Like the previous deer but here each bocage frond comprises three small leaflets. Such bocages occur on Walton-like figures but never on marked Walton figures. Price A.

Figure 119.156. Recumbent deer, to the right; with bocage. Probably made by Dale. H: ~5.4". Eight-petalled bocage flowers of this form consistently occur only on figures that link to Dale. Price A.

Figure 119.157. Recumbent deer, to the left; with bocage. H: ~5". Price A.

Figure 119.158. Recumbent stag, to the right; with bocage. H: ~4.8". Price A.

Figure 119.159. Recumbent stag, to the right; with bocage. H: ~4". Price A.

Figure 119.160. Recumbent stag, to the right; with bocage. H: 3.3". Price A. *Collection of Arnold and Barbara Berlin.*

Figure 119.161. Recumbent deer, to the right; with bocage. H: 2.8". The bocage has three-leaflet fronds. Flowers have six or eight petals. Price A. *Whitehall Antiques, Chapel Hill, North Carolina.*

Figure 119.162. Deer, reverse of previous example showing the three-leaflet bocage fronds. *Whitehall Antiques, Chapel Hill, North Carolina.*

Figure 119.163. Recumbent deer, to the right; with bocage. H: 3". Price A. *Peter Flemans.*

Figure 119.164. Deer, reverse of previous figure. The bocage fronds (each comprising seven tiny fern leaves) have been squeezed together to form a flattened structure. Bocage reattached. *Peter Flemans.*

Figure 119.165. Recumbent stag, to the right; with bocage. H: ~3.8". Price A.

Figure 119.166. Recumbent deer, to the right; with bocage. H: ~3.3". Unusual bocage leaves with an integral flower with black petals and a black stalk. Price A.

Figure 119.167. Recumbent deer, to the right; with bocage. H: ~3.3". The bocage is formed in one piece. Price A.

Figure 119.168. A pair of recumbent deer; with bocages. H: ~3.5". Price A.

Figure 119.169. Recumbent stag, to the left; with bocage. H: 3.5". Price A. *Andrew Dando Antiques.*

Figure 119.170. Recumbent doe, to the right. H: 2.3". Made without bocage. Price A. *Brighton and Hove Museums.*

Figure 119.171. Recumbent deer, to the left; with bocage. Marked "TITTENSOR". H: 3". This twelve-petalled bocage flower occurs only on other Tittensor figures and on figures made by Dale. Price A. *Image courtesy of The Potteries Museum & Art Gallery, Stoke-on-Trent, UK.*

Figure 119.172. Deer, reverse of previous figure showing the "TITTENSOR" mark. *Image courtesy of The Potteries Museum & Art Gallery, Stoke-on-Trent, UK.*

Figure 119.173. A pair of recumbent deer; with bocages. Possibly made by Salt. H: ~2.4". These figures and their bocages (with oak-leaf fronds and carnations) are in the same style as small Salt cows (fig. 118.87) and sheep (fig. 131.77). Price A.

Figure 119.174. Recumbent stag, to the left; with bocage. H: ~2.4". Like the previous stag but with a different bocage. Price A.

Figure 119.175. Recumbent stag, to the left; with bocage. H: 2.4". Apparently from the same molds as the previous small stags. Price A.

Figure 119.176. Stag, reverse of previous figure. This bocage occurs on other figures apparently from the same pot bank (Vol. 1, figs. 26.64, 28.43; Vol. 2, figs. 85.19, 108.37; and figs. 131.85, 131.179).

Figure 119.177. Recumbent stag, to the left. H: ~2.4". Made without bocage. Price A.

Figure 119.178. A pair of recumbent deer; with bocages. Attributed to "Sherratt." H: 2.8". Both bocages are flat and smooth on the reverse. Price A.

Figure 119.179. A pair of recumbent deer; with bocages. Attributed to "Sherratt." H: ~2.8". Like the previous pair, but the impressions on each base (a "Sherratt" feature) are better defined. Price A.

Figure 119.180. Recumbent deer, to the right; with bocage. H: 3.5". Unlike those in figure 119.179, this lacks "Sherratt" attributes and is almost certainly from another pot bank. Price A.

Figure 119.181. A pair of recumbent deer; with bocages. H: 3.5". Each bocage frond comprises three hawthorn leaves with integral flowers on the fronts of the fronds only. Price A. Peter Flemans

120. Dogs

Most early Staffordshire dogs are fashioned as setters, pointers, spaniels, and greyhounds. These dogs were prized hunting companions, and, until 1831, the law allowed only wealthy landed gentry to own them. Small dog figures are often modeled as pugs or the pampered pooches that belonged to refined ladies. The range of dog models reinforces the belief that well-to-do individuals were potters' target customers.

Most figures of dogs are easily recognizable as the breeds we know today. In sharp contrast are the rather fierce beasts portraying The Dog of Alcibiades (figs.120.1–3). The Dog of Alcibiades was the name given in the eighteenth century to a second-century sculpture of a dog without tail. Around 1755, an Englishman, Henry Constantine Jennings, saw this sculpture in a pile of rubble in Rome and bought it for £80. Noting the dog's broken tail, he named the dog for Alcibiades, a prominent fifth-century B.C.E. Athenian. Plutarch's biography of Alcibiades tells that he bought a beautiful dog with a large tail but had the dog's tail cut off so that people might direct all their anger at him for just this abuse. The sculpture Jennings salvaged is a Roman copy of a long-lost Hellenistic bronze from the second century B.C.E., and he, Jennings, shipped it back to England, where it became famous and was dubbed "Jennings' Dog." Many replicas were made—sometimes in pairs and always with intact tails. By 1778, Jennings had to sell the Dog to settle gambling debts, and it is now in the British Museum. Earthenware figures of The Dog of Alcibiades are reduced-scale depictions of the many popular sculptures of their day.

Figure 120.2. The Dog of Alcibiades, now in the British Museum. © *Marie-Lan Nguyen.*

Figure 120.1. The Dog of Alcibiades. Possibly made by Enoch Wood/Wood & Caldwell. H: 16.9". Price D. *Bonhams.*

Figure 120.3. The Dog of Alcibiades. H: ~16”. Made without the base. Price C. *Andrew Dando Antiques.*

Figure 120.4. Dog, after the Dog of Alcibiades. H: ~6”. Price B. *John Howard; www.antiquepottery.co.uk.*

Figure 120.5. Dog, after the Dog of Alcibiades. H: 4”. Price B.

Figure 120.6. Dog, after the Dog of Alcibiades. H: 4”. Like the previous dog but on a different base. Price B.

Figure 120.7. Dog, to the right. H: 6”, L: 9”. Price C. *Andrew Dando Antiques.*

Figure 120.8. Pointer, to the right; with bocage. H: 6.5”. Price B. *Brighton and Hove Museums.*

Figure 120.9. Setter, to the left; with bocage. H: 6.6”. Price C.

Figure 120.10. Pointer, to the right; setter, to the left, a pair. Possibly by Enoch Wood. L: ~6". The bases suggest an Enoch Wood attribution. Made without bocages. Price B. *Andrew Dando Antiques.*

Figure 120.11. Pointer, to the right. Possibly made by Enoch Wood. L: 6". Made without bocage. Price B. *John Howard; www.antiquepottery.co.uk.*

Figure 120.12. Pointer, to the right; with bocage. Probably made by Enoch Wood. H: 5.5". The base and bocage are typical of Enoch Wood. Companion to the following setter. Price C.

Figure 120.13. Excavated bocage from the Burslem Old Town Hall site, circa 1825–1830. The bocage fronds are formed like those on the previous pointer. These seven-leaflet fern fronds with six-petalled, star-like flowers are typical of Enoch Wood. *Image courtesy of The Potteries Museum & Art Gallery, Stoke-on-Trent, UK.*

Figure 120.14. Setter, to the left; with bocage. Probably made by Enoch Wood. H: 5.8". Companion to the previous pointer. The base and bocage are typical of Enoch Wood. Price B. *John Howard; www.antiquepottery.co.uk.*

Figure 120.15. Setter, to the left. Possibly made by Enoch Wood. L: 5.4". Made without bocage. Price B. *John Watson.*

Figure 120.16. Setter, to the left; with bocage. Attributed to Leather Leaf Group. H: 5.5". Bocage restored. Like the previous setter but formed from different molds. The characteristic flower on the base supports the attribution. Companion to the following setter. Price A.

Figure 120.17. Setter, to the right; with bocage. Attributed to Leather Leaf Group. H: 5.7". Companion to the previous setter. The curled bocage leaves and the flower and leaves on the base are typical of the Group. Price B.

Figure 120.18. Setter, reverse of previous figure showing typical Leather Leaf painting.

Figure 120.19. *POINTER, SETTER*. A pair of dogs; with bocages. H: 5.7"(L), 5.9"(R). These figures also occur with pink scrolling on the bases and with the dogs' patches painted black. Price C. *Elinor Penna.*

Figure 120.20. Pointer, to the right. H: 4.3", L: 7.5". Made without bocage. Price B. *Collection of Michael J. Smith.*

Figure 120.21. Fox with hen, to the right, greyhound with hare, to the left. A pair; with bocages. Attributed to Ralph Wood. H: ~6.7". The bocages support the attribution. Wood order books document the existence of this pair. Price C.

Figure 120.22. Greyhound with hare, to the left; with bocage. Attributed to Dudson. H: 7". With a typical Dudson bocage and characteristic x-sprigs on the base. Price B. *Brighton and Hove Museums.*

Figure 120.23. Greyhound, to the left. H: 4.8", L: 7". Made without bocage. Price B. *John Howard; www.antiquepottery.co.uk.*

Figure 120.24. Greyhound, to the left. H: 5", L: 7". Made without bocage. The same model as figure 120.23 but painted differently. Price B. *W. W. Warner Antiques.*

Figure 120.25. Pair of dogs, one holding a basket and the other a bag; with bocages. Attributed to Patriotic Group. H: 5.5". Other Patriotic Group animal figures are also on these bases. Price C. *A. Williamson.*

Figure 120.26. Pair of dogs, one holding a basket and the other a bag; with bocages. Attributed to Patriotic Group. H: ~5.6". Price C.

Figure 120.27. Dog holding a basket, to the left. H: ~3.5". Price B.

Figure 120.28. Pointer, to the left; with bocage. Attributed to Box Title Group. H: 5". The stalky bocage and two-tone painting of the base is typical of the Group. Price B.

Figure 120.29. Pair of dogs. H: ~5". Made without bocages. Price B.

Figure 120.30. Small dog, to the left. H: ~3". Made without bocage. Price A.

Figure 120.31. Small dog, to the right; with bocage. Impressed "WALTON". H: 4.6". This rare figure is a component of a Walton shooting garniture that can have as many as six pieces. Price B.

Figure 120.32. A four-piece shooting garniture comprising sportsman with dog, to the right; small dog, to the right; two small dogs, to the left; and sportsman, to the left. All with bocages. All marked "WALTON". H: 6.5" max. A figure of a small hare and a figure group of two pheasants can be added to this garniture (figs. 113.73, 130.2). Price E. *Jonathan Horne.*

Figure 120.33. Two small dogs on their hind legs. H: 3". Price B each.

Figure 120.35. Dog seated on a cushion, to the right. H: 4.6". Like the following dog but painted differently. Price A. *Elinor Penna.*

Figure 120.34. Pointer and setter, each seated on a tasseled cushion. Possibly made by Enoch Wood. H: 6.8". Traditionally attributed to Enoch Wood and derived from Ralph Wood models that occur decorated in colored glazes. Painted "27" beneath each. Price C.

Figure 120.36. Dog seated on a cushion, to the right. H: ~4.8". Price B.

Figure 120.37. Dog seated on a cushion, to the left. H: 4.8". Price A.
Barbara Gair; www.castle-antiques.com.

Figure 120.38. Dog seated, to the right. Possibly attributable to Patriotic Group. H: 3.2". The base suggests the attribution. Price B.

Figure 120.39. Dog seated, reverse of previous example.

Figure 120.40. Dog seated, to the right. H: 2.8". Price A. *Martyn Edgell Antiques Ltd.*

Figure 120.41. Dog seated, to the right. H: 4.5". Price A. *Andrew Dando Antiques.*

Figure 120.42. Dog seated, to the right; with bocage. Attributed to Dudson. H: ~3.5". Partial x-sprigs are on the base, and the bocage is consistent with Dudson. Price A.

Figure 120.43. Dog seated, to the left; with bocage. Attributed to Dudson. H: ~3.5". The bocage is specific to Dudson. Price A.

Figure 120.44. Dog seated, to the right; with bocage. Attributed to Leaf Mat Group. H: 2.8". Price A.

Figure 120.45. Dog seated, to the left; with bocage. H: ~3.2". These bocage fronds comprising three leaflets occur on other as yet unclassified figures from the same pot bank. Price A.

Figure 120.46. Dog seated, to the left; with bocage. H: ~3". The dog and the base are as figures 120.45 and 120.47, but the bocage differs. Price A.

Figure 120.47. Dog seated, to the left; with bocage. H: ~3". Like the previous two dogs but with a different bocage. Price A.

Figure 120.48. Dog seated, to the left. H: 2.8". Price A. *Aurea Carter Antiques.*

Figure 120.49. Dog seated on a tasseled cushion, to the left. H: 3.4". Price B.

Figure 120.50. Dog seated on a tasseled cushion, to the left. H: 3.4". Like the previous dog but painted differently. A pug facing right and on a cushion painted in these same colors has been recorded. Price B.

Figure 120.51. Dog seated on a tasseled cushion, to the left. H: 3.4". Like the previous two dogs, but this dog's face has been painted to make it look human. Price B. *John Howard; www.antiquepottery.co.uk.*

Figure 120.52. Pug seated on a tasseled cushion, to the right. H: 4.5". Larger and better defined than most pugs. Price B. *Gary Atkins.*

Figure 120.53. Pug seated on a tasseled cushion, to the right. H: ~3.8". Price A.

Figure 120.54. Pug seated on a tasseled cushion, to the right. H: 3.8". Price A. *Martyn Edgell Antiques Ltd.*

Figure 120.55. Pug seated on a tasseled cushion, to the right. H: 3.5". Price A. *www.madelena.com.*

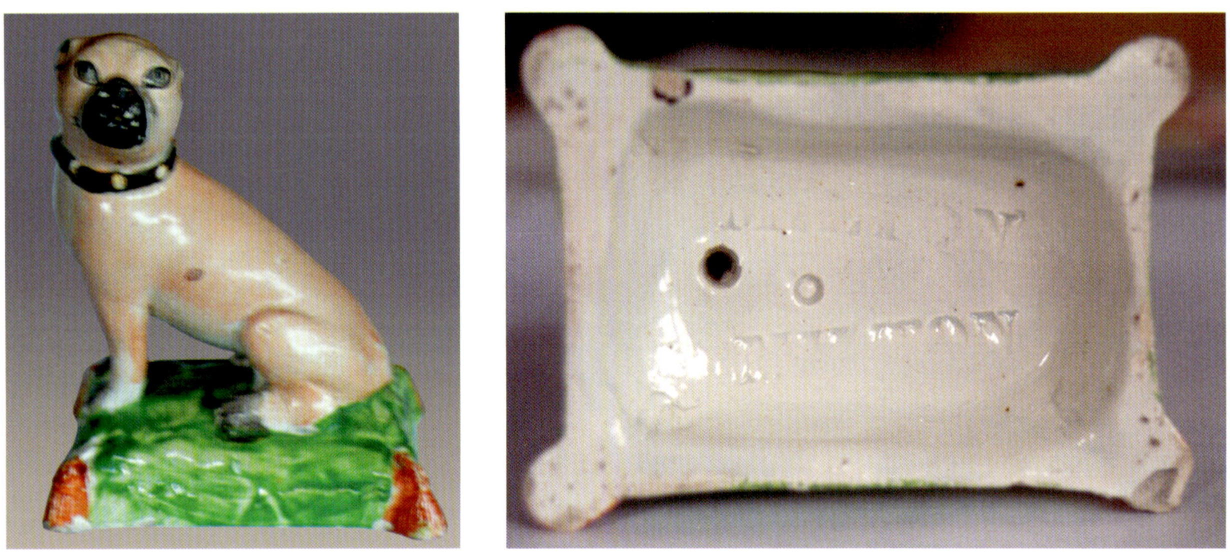

Figure 120.56. Pug seated on a tasseled cushion, to the left. H: ~3.7". Impressed "MILTON" twice beneath. The only recorded figure with this mark. Price A.

Figure 120.57. Pug seated on a tasseled cushion, to the left. H: ~4". Price A.

Figure 120.58. Dog seated to the left. H: ~3.5". Price A.

Figure 120.59. *ROVER &.* Recumbent dog, to the right; with bocage. Attributed to "Sherratt." H: 4.4". A rare figure, sometimes found untitled. Pairs with the following figure, *VAL LAY*. Price C.

Figure 120.60. *VAL LAY.* Recumbent dog with suckling pups, to the left; with bocage. Attributed to "Sherratt." H: 4.1". The only recorded example. Pairs with the previous figure to read *ROVER & VAL LAY*. Price C.

Figure 120.61. *MIND DASH*. Recumbent greyhound, to the left; with bocage. Attributed to "Sherratt." H: 6". The only known example. Price C.

Figure 120.62. Recumbent spaniel, to the right. H: 4.8", L: 8.8". Price D. *John Howard; www.antiquepottery.co.uk.*

Figure 120.63. Recumbent dog with a puppy, to the right. H: 4.5", L: 7". The only known example. Price C. *The William Herbert and Nancy Hunt Collection.*

Figure 120.64. Recumbent dog, possibly a wolf, to the right. L: 6". Feet probably lost from base. Price B. *John Howard; www.antiquepottery.co.uk.*

Figure 120.65. Recumbent greyhound, to the right. L: 6". Price B. *John Howard; www.antiquepottery.co.uk.*

Figure 120.66. Recumbent greyhound, to the right, with bocage socket. L: ~6.5". This socket once held a detachable bocage, now lost. Dale made bocages to fit into sockets, but the figure shows no characteristics of his work. Price B. *Elinor Penna.*

Figure 120.67. Recumbent setter, to the right. L: ~6.2". Like the following setter and possibly made by Enoch Wood. Price B. *John Howard; www.antiquepottery.co.uk.*

Figure 120.68. Recumbent setter, to the right. Possibly made by Enoch Wood. L: 6.2". The base is formed and decorated in the style of Enoch Wood. Pairs with the following dog. Price B. *Elinor Penna.*

Figure 120.69. Recumbent dog, to the left. Possibly made by Enoch Wood. L: 6.2". Pairs with the previous setter and has a typical Enoch Wood base. Price B. *Elinor Penna.*

Figure 120.70. Pair of recumbent greyhounds. L: 6.6". Price C. *Elinor Penna.*

Figure 120.71. Recumbent greyhound, to the left. L: 6.5". Price B.

Figure 120.72. Recumbent setter, to the right. L: ~ 6". Possibly a companion to the following greyhound. Price B.

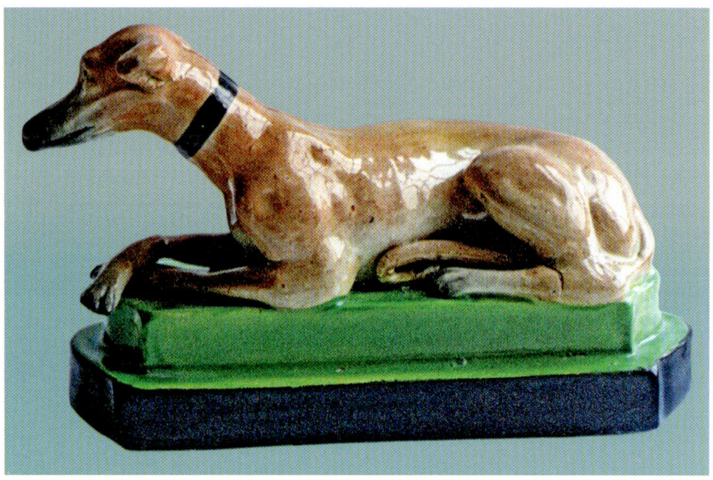

Figure 120.73. Recumbent greyhound, to the left. L: ~6". Possibly a companion to the previous setter. Price B.

Figure 120.74. Recumbent greyhound, to the left. L: 7". This dog is not as snuggly placed on the base as previous similarly styled greyhounds. Also, the base is different. Price B. *Collection of Michael J. Smith.*

Figure 120.75. Recumbent setter, to the right. L: ~7". This dog is not as snuggly placed on the base as previous similarly styled setters. Possibly a companion to the previous greyhound. Price B.

Figure 120.76. Recumbent dog, to the right. L: 6.5". Formed from simple molds and entirely open beneath. Price B.

Figure 120.77. Recumbent dog, to the right. L: 3.5". Price B. *John Howard; www.antiquepottery.co.uk.*

Figure 120.78. Recumbent dog, to the left. L: 3.4". Price A. *Brighton and Hove Museums.*

Figure 120.79. Recumbent dog, to the right. L: 2.7". Price A. *Elinor Penna.*

Figure 120.80. Dog, to the right. Attributed to "Sherratt." H: 1.9", L: 2". The sprigging on the base matches the sprigging on the bases of other small "Sherratt" figures. Possibly intended to pair with the following dog. Price A.

Figure 120.81. Dog, to the left. Attributed to "Sherratt." H: 1.7", L: 1.7". Possibly intended to pair with the previous dog. Price A.

Figure 120.82. Dog, to the right. Attributed to "Sherratt." H: 2", L: 1.5". In the same style as the previous small "Sherratt" dogs (figs. 120.80–81) and with a similar naïve appeal. Price A.

Figure 120.83. Dog with sheep; with spill vase. H: 4". Unusual and finely potted. Slightly larger spill vases with only sheep occur in much the same style (figs, 131.213–215). Price B.

Figure 120.84. Two dogs; with spill vase. H: 4". From the same pot bank as the previous spill vase and uses many of the same molds. Price B.

Figure 120.85. Box with coat of arms with Prince of Wales feathers, a dog atop the lid. Attributed to "Sherratt." H: 4.2". The dog, the coat of arms, and the sprigging flanking the front are on other "Sherratt" examples. The box is painted like tables on some "Sherratt" groups. Price C.

121. Dogs with People

Numerous earthenware figure groups include a small dog upon their bases, reflecting the centrality of dogs to English domestic life. Figures of hunters, dandies, musicians, and family groups are among the many examples that include a little dog and are shown elsewhere in this work. In particular, figures of a boy playing with his dog that pair with a girl with a sheep are shown among the shepherds and shepherdesses in Volume 1, chapter 27.

The figures below give glimpses of people interacting with dogs in ways that may seem strange today. In particular, the concept of riding a dog is alien to us, but around 1800, the dog was viewed as a working animal. At that time, draught dogs were in vogue. Dogs were cheaper to feed and replace than horses, and dog carts, unlike horse-drawn vehicles, did not pay road tolls. Children and the aged rode in dog carts, and dog teams dragged weighty commercial merchandise.

Figure 121.1. Lady with child astride a dog and another child; with bocage. H: 9.4". A companion group shows children giving alms to an elderly man (Vol. 4, fig. 145.3). Both groups have this stunning bocage, which occurs rarely and only on unmarked figures. Price D. *W. W. Warner Antiques.*

Figure 121.2. Lady with child astride a dog and another child; with bocage. H: 9.2", L: 9.2". Like the previous example, but the bocage comprises three-leaflet fronds. Price C. *Elinor Penna.*

Figure 121.3. Lady with child astride a dog and another child; with bocage. H: ~9.2", L: ~9.2". Like the previous example, but the bocage has five-leaflet fronds. The boy is not original to this group and is of the incorrect form. Price B.

Figure 121.4. Lady with child astride a dog and another child. H: 8". Made without bocage. Price C. *Elinor Penna.*

Figure 121.5. Lady with child riding a dog. H: 7.5". Uses some of the same molds as the larger groups previously shown, with minor modifications. This model was always made without bocage. Price B. *Andrew Dando Antiques.*

Figure 121.6. Child astride a dog. H: 4.9". Known from only this example. Bocage lost. Price A. *Elinor Penna.*

Figure 121.7. Child astride dog. H: 2.8". Price A. *Elinor Penna.*

Figure 121.8. Boy with dog, girl with cat, a pair. H: ~6". Price B.

Figure 121.9. Boy with dog. H: ~6". Like the previous boy, but here the mound beneath his feet is narrower than the square base, which is painted differently. Price A. *Andrew Dando Antiques.*

Figure 121.10. Boy with dog. H: 5.2". Pairs with a girl with a cat (fig. 117.3). Both are in a late eighteenth-century palette. Price A.

Figure 121.11. Boy with dog. H: 7.9". Pairs with a girl holding a cat (fig. 117.1). Price A. *Brighton and Hove Museums.*

Figure 121.12. Gentleman with dog. Height not known. The pink luster base is unusual. Price A.

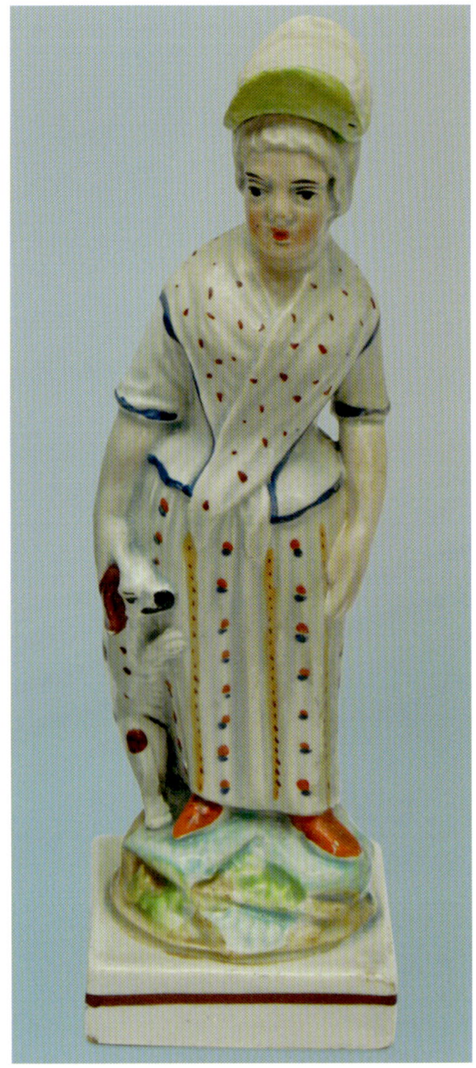

Figure 121.13. Lady with dog. Attributed to Ralph Wood III. H: 5.5". The painting of the base (lines on three sides only) and mound and the formation of the base support the attribution. See Volume 1, figure 30.16 for the companion figure. Price A. *Michael Goodacre.*

Figure 121.14. Boy with dog. H: 2.9". Possibly attributable to "Sherratt." The sprigged pattern on the base occurs on some other small "Sherratt" figures. Price A. *Collection of Arnold and Barbara Berlin.*

Figure 121.15. Girl with dog. Possibly attributable to "Sherratt." H: 2.9". The base is suggestive of "Sherratt." Price A. *www.madelena.com.*

Figure 121.16. Lady seated with a dog in her lap. H: 2.7". Similarly styled figures of a lady holding a cat usually are decorated in underglaze colors. Price A.

Figure 121.17. Lady with dog, gentleman sleeping; with spill vase. Attributed to Patriotic Group. H: ~6". The flower applied to the base is specific to the Group. Price A.

Figure 121.18. Lady with dog; with spill vase. Marked "WALTON". H: 6". Companion to the following spill vase. Price A. *Peter Flemans.*

Figure 121.19. Gentleman sleeping, with dog; with spill vase. Marked "WALTON". H: 6". Companion to the previous spill vase. Price A. *Peter Flemans.*

Figure 121.20. Boy sitting with begging dog. H: 6.8", L: 7.2". Modeled with a flat back and mounted on a rectangular base for stability. The back is undecorated. Fewer than a dozen groups with flat unpainted backs are recorded, and this is the largest. Price B. *John Howard; www.antiquepottery.co.uk.*

Figure 121.21. Boy sitting with begging dog. H: 6.7". Like the previous example but decorated differently. Price B. *Brighton and Hove Museums.*

Figure 121.22. Boy sitting with dog; with bocage. H: ~5". Price A.

Figure 121.23. Gentleman with dog. H: 4.7". Price A. *Peter Flemans.*

Figure 121.24. Gentleman with dog. Impressed "TITTENSOR". H: 4". Price B.

Figure 121.25. Gentleman with dog, reverse of previous example showing the Tittensor mark.

122. Elephants

From the late eighteenth century, traveling menageries introduced elephants to people across Britain. In those years, elephants were much in the news. In 1826, the horrific slaughter of Chunee, a beloved London menagerie elephant, provoked public outrage; in 1828, an elephant act debuted at Astley's circus; and in 1829, an elephant appeared on the London stage for the first time. Nonetheless, earthenware elephants are particularly rare.

Figures of elephants are all exceptionally interesting. Possibly the earliest elephant model of this period is a large free-standing elephant decorated in colored glazes and attributed to Ralph Wood. Ralph Wood may also have made the enamel-painted look-alikes of this elephant (fig. 122.1) but there is no basis for definitive attribution. Another early elephant was originally modeled to serve as a teapot (fig. 122.3). Similar color-glazed examples in the Weldon Collection each have a large monkey perched on the lid, and a similar teapot in the Metropolitan Museum of Art has three small coolies atop the lid.[1]

Large elephants with crenellated howdahs atop their backs (figs. 122.4–9) are believed to date from the nineteenth century. Elephants like this are rare, and all recorded examples are shown on these pages. The motif of a castellated elephant has been used for centuries in the arms of the city of Coventry and as the emblem of London's Cutlers' Company. Also, a castellated elephant traditionally appeared on menagerie show cloths. In addition to the figures shown, a smaller, cruder elephant with a short castle on its back has been recorded. That elephant stood on a raised rectangular base with sloping walls decorated with fan-shaped motifs.[2]

The very smallest elephants measure just 2" in height, or somewhat taller if made with a bocage (figs. 122.11–15). These tiny elephants link directly to a figure and shard from the Enoch Wood excavations at the Burslem Old Town Hall site (Volume 1, page 23).

Figure 122.1. Elephant. Probably made by Ralph Wood. H: ~7", L: ~9". Price E. *John Howard; www.antiquepottery.co.uk.*

Figure 122.2. Two elephants, enamel-painted (L), color-glazed (R). Probably made by Ralph Wood (L), attributed to Ralph Wood (R). H: ~7", L: ~9". The elephant in figure 122.1 is shown alongside a color-glazed elephant that appears to be from the same molds. *Andrew Dando Antiques.*

Figure 122.3. Elephant formed as a teapot, lid lost. H: ~8.5". The enameling is consistent with that used by Ralph Wood and other late eighteenth-century manufacturers. Price B.

Figure 122.4. Elephant with howdah and mahout. H: 9". The howdah is open at the top, allowing it to serve as a spill vase. Price E.

Figure 122.5. Detail of the mahout in figure 122.4.

Figure 122.6. Elephant with howdah and mahout. H: 9". Like the elephant in figure 122.4 but on a different base. Price E. *Brighton and Hove Museums.*

Figure 122.7. Elephant with howdah and mahout. H: 8.6". Like the previous model, but an opening in the howdah has transformed the group into a watch stand. Price D.

Figure 122.8. Elephant with howdah and mahout. H: ~9". The elephant, the mahout, and the howdah are formed from different molds than were used for the previous examples. Price D. *Photograph Courtesy of Sotheby's, Inc. © 2014.*

Figure 122.9. Elephant with howdah and mahout. H: 9". This albino elephant has a black rider. Formed from the same molds as figure 122.8. Price D.

Figure 122.10. Elephant, to the right; with bocage. H: ~7". Bocage restored. Price B.

Figure 122.11. Small elephant, to the right; with bocage. Attributed to Enoch Wood. H: ~4.4". The palm bocage fronds and the elephant match an Enoch Wood figure and fragments excavated from the Burslem Old Town Hall site. Price B.

Figure 122.12. Pair of small elephants; with bocages. Attributed to Enoch Wood. H: 4.2" (L), 4.4"(R). Like the previous elephant and with Enoch Wood bocages. Price C.

Figure 122.13. Small elephant, to the right. Attributed to Enoch Wood. H: 2". Made without bocage. Like figures 122.11-12 and on a typical Enoch Wood base. Price B. *John Howard; www.antiquepottery.co.uk.*

Figure 122.14. Small elephant, to the right; with bocage. Attributed to Enoch Wood. H: ~6.4". The elephant is larger than previous small elephants. The base and bocage are consistent with an Enoch Wood attribution. Price B.

Figure 122.15. Two small elephants shown in figures 122.11 and 122.14. Side by side, the size discrepancy is significant.

123. Foxes

By the early 1800s, the popularity of fox hunting had decimated England's fox population. Foxes had become so scarce that it was necessary to kennel them for the hunt and, rather than kill them, to bag them afterward for reuse. Fox hunting had its ugly side: many small farmers leased their land, but the foxes on it remained the property of landlords, who retained the right to kill them. Faced with destruction of their livestock by foxes and the trampling of their crops by affluent hunters, tenant farmers resorted to illegally killing the foxes that plagued them, and courts dispensed harsh punishment when they were caught.

Figure 123.2. Fox with fowl; with bocage. Attributed to "Sherratt." L: ~7". The floral sprigs applied to the base are specific to "Sherratt." Price B.

Figure 123.1. Fox with fowl, greyhound with hare, both with bocages. L: 7.2". Attributed to Ralph Wood. The bocage is specific to Ralph Wood. Wood order books of 1786 verify the production of these models. Price C. *Jonathan Horne.*

Figure 123.3. Fox with fowl; with bocage. L: ~7". From a different pot bank to previous examples. Price B.

Figure 123.4. Fox with fowl; with bocage. H: 6". A companion greyhound with this bocage and with similar leaves strewn on the base is recorded. Price B. *Brighton and Hove Museums.*

Figure 123.5. Fox with fowl; with bocage. Attributed to Patriotic Group. H: 6.5". The floral sprig alongside the fowl is specific to the Patriotic Group. Price B. *The William Herbert and Nancy Hunt Collection.*

Figure 123.6. Fox with fowl, reverse of previous figure. The bocage fronds (each with one leaflet atop five) are consistent with the attribution. *The William Herbert and Nancy Hunt Collection.*

Figure 123.7. Fox fleeing with a goose in its mouth; with spill vase. H: 4.9". Spill vases of this form, predominantly with animal subjects, are apparently from the same pot bank (figs. 126.136–137, 119.79–80, 131.94–95, and Vol. 4, fig. 197.79). Price B. *Brighton and Hove Museums.*

Figure 123.8. Fox, seated. H: 4.1". Like the contemporary Derby fox. Price B. *Brighton and Hove Museums.*

Figure 123.9. Fox devouring a large fowl; with bocage. Attributed to Ralph Wood. H: 5.3". The bocage and color palette are typical of Ralph Wood. Price A. *Woolley and Wallis Salisbury Salerooms Ltd.*

Figure 123.10. Fox. L: 2.7". Price A. *John B. Watson.*

124. Goats

By the nineteenth century, goats had not attained the status of other livestock. For this reason, figures of goats are far less common than are figures of other farm animals. Sometimes, larger figural groups—particularly those incorporating musicians—include a small goat, but stand-alone figures of goats are unusual.

Figure 124.1. Goat with kid, to the right; with bocage. Attributed to Ralph Wood; impressed "150". H: ~5.8". Bocage restored. This figure is also recorded without an impressed number and with an original bocage typical of Ralph Wood. Price A.

Figure 124.2. Goat with kid, to the left; with bocage. Possibly made by Ralph Wood. H: ~5.8". Price A.

Figure 124.3. Goat with kid, to the right; with bocage. H: 7.6". Price A. *Collection of Michael J. Smith.*

Figure 124.4. Goat with kid, to the right; with bocage. Attributed to Starred Anthemion Group. H: ~6". A ewe with the same bocage has been recorded. Price A.

Figure 124.5. Goat with kid, to the right. H: ~4.5". The bocage is lost. The goat and kid appear to be from the same molds as those in the previous example. Price A.

Figure 124.6. Goat with kid, to the right. Probably made by Enoch Wood. H. 3.9". The bocage is lost. Matches a figure found at the Burslem Old Town Hall site associated with Enoch Wood. Price A.

Figure 124.7. Goat with kid, to the right; with bocage. Attributed to Enoch Wood. H: 5.6". Like the previous figure and on the same base. The bocage fronds (one leaflet atop four others) are a typical Enoch Wood form. Price A.

Figure 124.8. Goat with kid, to the right; with bocage. Attributed to Patriotic Group. H: 5". The bocage flowers are characteristic of the Group. Price A.

Figure 124.9. Goat with kid, to the right; with bocage. Attributed to Patriotic Group. H: ~5". Like the previous goat but with a different bocage that is consistent with the attribution. Price A.

Figure 124.10. Goat with kid, to the right; with bocage. H: ~5". Restoration to bocage. Price A.

Figure 124.11. Goat with kid, to the right; with bocage. H: ~5". Restored bocage. Price A.

Figure 124.12. Goat with kid, to the right; with bocage. H: ~5". Price A.

Figure 124.13. Goat with kid, to the right; with bocage. H: 5". Restored bocage. Price A. *Barbara Gair; www.castle-antiques.com.*

Figure 124.16. Recumbent goat, to the left; with bocage. H: ~3". Possibly a Ralph Wood bocage, with restoration. Price A.

Figure 124.19. Recumbent goat, to the left; with spill vase. H: 3.1". Pairs with a similar spill vase with a sheep (fig. 131.191). Price A.

Figure 124.14. Goat to the right; with spill vase. H: 3.3". Price A. *Andrew Dando Antiques.*

Figure 124.17. Recumbent goat, to the left. L: 2.1". Made without bocage. Price A. *Aurea Carter Antiques.*

Figure 124.20. Goat, to the left. Probably made at the Kirkaldy pot bank, near Glasgow. H: 8.5". Made without bocage. With under-glaze and some enamel colors. Goats of this sort are associated with the Scottish potteries. Price C. *John Howard; www.antiquepottery.co.uk.*

Figure 124.15. Recumbent goat, to the right. H: 6.3", L: 7.6". Price B. *Andrew Dando Antiques.*

Figure 124.18. Recumbent goat, to the left; with spill vase. H: ~3". Price A.

Figure 124.21. Goat, to the left. Probably made at the Kirkaldy pot bank or at one of the other Scottish potteries. H: ~8.5". Made without bocage. With under-glaze and some enamel colors. Price C. *John Howard; www.antiquepottery.co.uk.*

125. Horses and Donkeys

Figures of horses and their riders (shown elsewhere) are among the most spectacular earthenware creations, but solitary horses are quite rare. The largest horses measure around seventeen inches in height and are believed to have been made for saddlers and other tradesmen to use in window displays (figs. 125.3–4). These horses are technical accomplishments in that their thin earthenware legs must support a large body. Most are decorated in under-glaze colors and are traditionally attributed to the Leeds Pottery. The earliest examples stand on flat bases, usually with chamfered corners and a moulded leaf frieze around the edge, and one is recorded incised "J. Metcalf 1821".[1] This thin base form was soon found to distort in the kiln, so it was quickly replaced with a higher base.

Figure 125.1. Prancing horse. Possibly made by Ralph Wood. H: 11", L: 9". An example of this figure decorated in colored glazes is in the Metropolitan Museum of Art (43.100.14). Price E. *The William Herbert and Nancy Hunt Collection.*

Figure 125.2. Prancing horse, to the right. Height not known. Price C.

125.3. Horse, to the right. Attributed to the Leeds Pottery. H: 17". With some under-glaze colors. Price G. *Elinor Penna.*

Figure 125.4. Horse, to the right. Attributed to the Leeds Pottery. H: 16.7". The paint was applied to unglazed earthenware to simulate marble. In 1848 (and possibly earlier), this horse stood in the shop window of Joseph Robinson at 120 Domestic Street, Holbeck, an area on the doorstep of the Leeds Pottery. Price G. *The William Herbert and Nancy Hunt Collection.*

Figure 125.5. Horse, to the left; with bocage. Attributed to Enoch Wood/Wood & Caldwell. H: 10.5", L: 13". The bocage is typical of Enoch Wood. Companion to a similarly styled cow (fig. 118.9). Price D. *The William Herbert and Nancy Hunt Collection.*

Figure 125.6. Horse, to the left; with spill vase. Impressed "WOOD & CALDWELL BURSLEM". H: 8.6", L~13". Pairs with a similarly styled cow, marked in the same way (fig. 118.5). Price D.

Figure 125.7. Race horse. H: 7.2". The horse is attired to arrive at the racecourse and wears a training blanket, saddle, and ankle guards. The owner's initials ("S" and "G") are painted on the blanket. Price F. *Bonhams*.

Figure 125.8. Horses, a pair; with bocages. Attributed to Patriotic Group. H: ~5.8". This base is also used for Patriotic Group lions, leopards, and dogs. The bocage flowers are specific to the Group. Price C.

Figure 125.9. Horse, to the left; with bocage. Attributed to Patriotic Group. H: ~5.8". Price B.

Figure 125.10. Horse, to the left; with bocage. Attributed to Patriotic Group. H: ~5.8". Price B.

Figure 125.11. Donkey, to the left; with bocage. Attributed to Patriotic Group. H: ~5.8". On the same distinctive base as previous figures, but the animal is a donkey. Price B.

Figure 125.12. Recumbent horse, to the right. L: ~7". Known only from this example. Possibly a unicorn, because a similar figure with a single horn is rcorded. A recumbent lion on a similar base is documented. Price B.

Figure 125.13. Prancing horses. H: 5.8", L: 7.5". A rare figure. The back is flat and unpainted. Price B. *John Howard; www.antiquepottery.co.uk.*

126. Lions, Leopards, Tigers, and Panthers

Earthenware lions often have particularly engaging, human faces. This, coupled with the lion's role as England's national symbol, makes them popular, even though they are the commonest of the clay cats. Other large felines are few and far between, and most are avidly sought by collectors.

Lions of all sizes are frequently modeled standing with one front paw placed on a ball. This pose is after that of the lions at the Loggia dei Lanzi, Florence. One Florentine lion is of ancient origin; its mate is sixteenth century. The Bow factory mimicked these lions circa 1750, as did Chelsea thereafter, and Staffordshire potters followed suit. Many recumbent lions, on the other hand, may be modeled after a source closer to home. In the eighteenth century, the sculptor John Bacon made a recumbent dog-like lion and a lioness for Heaton Hall, Manchester. This lion probably inspired recumbent earthenware lions with appealing expressions. Enoch Wood/Wood & Caldwell made the most well-known lions of this form, and lions by Walton and others are styled similarly.

Felines were especially newsworthy in the early nineteenth century. In July 1825, the menagerist George Wombwell baited his famous menagerie lions, Wallace and Nero. Only a handful of figures titled NERO and WALLACE memorialize the animals that each defended the title of King of the Beasts in successive bloody contests (figs. 126.48–51). Shown elsewhere are figures depicting gruesome attacks in which lions and tigers killed people (chapter 136) and lions accompanied by unicorns (Volume 2, chapter 63).

Figure 126.1. Two lions, each with a paw on a ball. L: 13.3". Lions posed thus are after the lions at the Loggia dei Lanzi, Florence. Price D. *The William Herbert and Nancy Hunt Collection.*

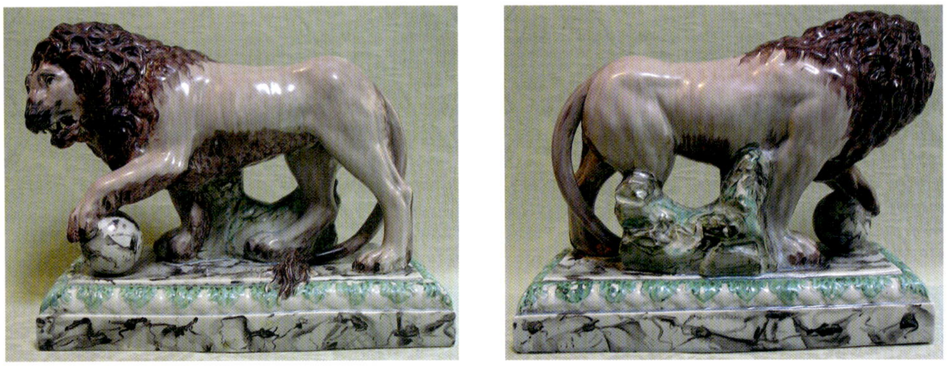

Figure 126.2. Lion with a paw on a ball, to the left. Impressed "WEDGWOOD". L: 11.4". Ralph Wedgwood was a skilled copier, and this lion is indistinguishable from unmarked lions probably made by other pot banks. Price B. *Bob Mores at Nestegg Antiques.*

Figure 126.3. Lion with a paw on a ball and a small lion, to the left. L: 13". Price D. The small lion on the base is an unusual touch. See also figure 126.12. *The William Herbert and Nancy Hunt Collection.*

Figure 126.4. Lion with a paw on a ball, to the left. L: 12.1". Price B. *Northeast Auctions.*

Figure 126.5. Lion with a paw on a ball, to the left. H: 8.5", L: 11.6". Note the flowers on the base. Price B. *www.madelena.com.*

Figure 126.7. Lion with a paw on a ball, to the right. L: ~12". Note the unusual floral base. Price B.

Figure 126.6. Pair of lions, each with a paw on a ball. L: ~12". Price C. *John Howard; www.antiquepottery.co.uk.*

Figure 126.8. Lion with a paw on a ball, to the right. H: 8.7", L: 11". The ball is painted to simulate the globe. Price B. *Cynthia Bell Wolodkin, Golden Retriever Antiques.*

Figure 126.9. Lion with a paw on a ball, to the right. L: 11". This lion differs from previous examples in that it has a quite human face and a dog-like expression. Price C. *Pook & Pook, Inc., Auctioneers & Appraisers.*

Figure 126.11. Lion with a paw on a ball, to the left. L: 13". The base is molded differently from that on previous examples. Price C. *John Howard; www.antiquepottery.co.uk.*

Figure 126.10. Lion with a paw on a ball, to the right. L: 11". Price C. *John Howard; www.antiquepottery.co.uk.*

Figure 126.12. Lion with a paw on a ball alongside a diminutive lion posed similarly, both to the left. L: 12.4". The most charming of the big lion examples. Price D. *Image courtesy of The Potteries Museum & Art Gallery, Stoke-on-Trent, UK.*

Figure 126.13. Pair of lions, each with a paw on a ball. L: ~12". Note the use of pink luster. Price B.

Figure 126.14. Lion with a paw on a ball, to the left. L: ~12". Note the silver luster ball. Price B. *Andrew Dando Antiques.*

Figure 126.15. Lion with a paw on a ball, to the right. L: 14.5". Price C. *Photograph Courtesy of Sotheby's, Inc. © 2014.*

Figure 126.16. Lion with a paw on a ball, to the left. H: 5.3". Price C.

Figure 126.17. Lion with a paw on a ball, to the left. Made by Benjamin Plant and incised "B. Plant Lane End". L: 15.5". Note the luster ball and the unusual decoration atop the base. Price C. *Jonathan Horne.*

Figure 126.18. Lion with a barrel in its mouth and a paw on a ball, to the left. L: 12.1". "R" is painted on the side of the barrel. Price B. *Elinor Penna.*

Figure 126.19. *THE RORAN LION*. Lion with a paw on a ball, to the left. Attributed to "Sherratt." L: 13.2". Possibly intended to stand with *THE DEATH OF MUŃROW*. Recorded untitled and titled *THE RORING LION*. Also occurs on "Sherratt" mound base and brown clawed table base. Price C. *The William Herbert and Nancy Hunt Collection.*

Figure 126.20. *THE RORAN LION.* Lion with a paw on a ball, to the left. Attributed to "Sherratt." L: ~13.4". This black lion is very unusual. Possibly stands with *THE DEATH OF MUNROW* group with a black tiger (fig. 135.9). A similar dark lion on a pink base is of much later manufacture. Price C. *Bonhams.*

Figure 126.21. Lion mauling a deer. L: 13". Attributed to "Sherratt." Known from only this example. The floral sprigs on the base are specific to "Sherratt." Price D.

Figure 126.22. Tiger mauling a lamb. Attributed to "Sherratt." L: 7.3". Uses some of the same molds as used for the "Sherratt" group with a tiger mauling a woman and child (fig. 136.1). Price D. *© Christie's Images Limited 2014.*

Figure 126.23. Tiger mauling a lamb. Attributed to "Sherratt." L: 8". Like the previous example but on a different "Sherratt" base. Price D.

Figure 126.24. Pair of lions, each with a paw on a ball. Attributed to "Sherratt." L: 6.8". The bases are specific to "Sherratt." Smaller than the previous lions. A pair is difficult to obtain, and single examples are always in demand. Price D.

Figure 126.25. Lion with a paw on a ball, to the right. Attributed to "Sherratt." L: 6.8". Like figure 126.24 but with pink luster. A "Sherratt" deer (fig. 119.53) stands on a base painted in this manner. Price C.

Figure 126.26. Lion with a paw on a ball, to the left. Possibly attributable to "Sherratt." H: 5.3". Like previous "Sherratt" examples but painted in an atypical manner. Price B. *Elinor Penna.*

Figure 126.27. Lion with a paw on a ball, to the right. Attributed to "Sherratt." The rainbow base is typical of "Sherratt." Tail probably restored. Price C.

Figure 126.28. Lion with a paw on a ball, to the right. Attributed to "Sherratt." L: ~7". A typical "Sherratt" feathered base. Price C. *John Howard; www.antiquepottery.co.uk.*

Figure 126.29. Lion with a paw on a ball, to the right. Attributed to "Sherratt." L: ~7". A typical "Sherratt" brown table base. Companion to the following lion, but the tails are placed differently. A similar lion titled THE LION is documented. Price C. *Collection of Barbara Hunt Crow.*

Figure 126.30. Lion with a paw on a ball, to the left. Attributed to "Sherratt." H: ~8". Companion to the previous lion. Price C. *Collection of Michael J. Smith.*

Figure 126.31. Lion with a paw on a ball, to the left. Attributed to "Sherratt." L: ~6.8". This base is less distinctive than previous "Sherratt" bases, but it occurs on many other "Sherratt" figures. Price C. *John Howard; www.antiquepottery.co.uk.*

Figure 126.32. Lion with a paw on a ball, to the left. Attributed to "Sherratt." L: ~6.8". Price C.

Figure 126.33. Lion with a paw on a ball, to the right; with bocage. Attributed to "Sherratt." H: ~6.5". The floral sprigs applied to the base are specific to "Sherratt." Decorated in the turquoise palette that "Sherratt" sometimes used. Companion to the following lion. Price C.

Figure 126.34. Lion with a paw on a ball, to the left; with bocage. Attributed to "Sherratt." H: 6.5". Companion to the previous lion but with different bocage flowers. Price B. *John Howard; www.antiquepottery.co.uk.*

Figure 126.35. Assembled pair of lions, each with a paw on a ball; with bocage. Attributed to "Sherratt." H: 6.5". The sprigs applied to the base are specific to "Sherratt." Price C each. *John Howard; www.antiquepottery.co.uk.*

Figure 126.36. Lion with a paw on a ball, to the left; with bocage. H: ~6". Like the previous lion but a little smaller and heavier. Importantly, the "Sherratt"-like sprigs, instead of being applied separately, are integral to the base. Possibly this figure was modeled from a "Sherratt" figure. Price B.

Figure 126.37. Lion with a paw on a ball, to the right; with bocage. Attributed to "Sherratt." H: 7.7". This waisted base is characteristic of "Sherratt." Companion to the following lion. Price C. *Image courtesy of The Potteries Museum & Art Gallery, Stoke-on-Trent, UK.*

Figure 126.38. Lion with a paw on a ball, to the left; with bocage. Attributed to "Sherratt." H: ~7". Price C.

Figure 126.39. Lion with a paw on a ball, to the right. H: ~6". Bases with shield motifs occur on Flight and Return figure groups (Vol. 2, figs. 93.23–24) and on figure 199.25 in Volume 4. Price A. *Collection of Barbara Hunt Crow.*

Figure 126.40. Pair of lions, each with a paw on a ball. L: 5.8". These lions have particularly animated expressions. Price D.

Figure 126.41. Pair of lions, each with a paw on a ball. L: ~6". Price C. *John Howard; www.antiquepottery.co.uk.*

Figure 126.42. Pair of lions, each with a paw on a ball. L: ~6". Price C.

Figure 126.43. Pair of lions, each with a paw on a ball. L: 6". On colorful oblong bases that differ in form from those of the previous pair. Price C. *Collection of Michael J. Smith.*

Figure 126.44. Pair of lions, each with a paw on a ball. H: 5.6", L: 6". Like the previous pair but painted quite differently. Price C. *Elinor Penna.*

Figure 126.45. Lion with a paw on a ball, to the left. L: 6". Price B. *John Howard; www.antiquepottery.co.uk.*

Figure 126.46. Lion, to the left. H: 5.5", L: 6.5". Price B. *John Howard; www.antiquepottery.co.uk.*

Figure 126.47. Lions, a pair. L: ~6.5". Price C.

Figure 126.48. *WALLACE, NERO*. A pair of lions, each with a paw on a ball, bocages lost. L: 6.5". Engaging, anthropomorphic faces. The only recorded pair of the menagerie lions baited in July 1825. An assembled pair, bocages lost, is in John Hall, *Staffordshire Portrait Figures*, 68–69. Price D.

Figure 126.49. *WALLACE*. Lion with a paw on a ball, to the right; with bocage. Attributed to Hall. H: 6.4". These bocage flowers are linked to Hall. The bocage fronds and flowers are painted in a manner suggestive of Hall. Companion to the following lion. Price C. © *Christie's Images Limited 2014*.

Figure 126.50. *NERO*. Lion with a paw on a ball, to the left; with bocage. H: ~6.5". Companion to the previous lion and probably made by Hall but with no definitive Hall features. Price C.

Figure 126.51. *NERO*. Lion on a raised base. Made in Scotland. H: 8.7". A similar untitled lion is recorded. The color palette and form of the base point to a Scottish origin. Price D. *Photograph Courtesy of Sotheby's, Inc. © 2014*.

Figure 126.52. Lion, probably intended to be the famous Nero. H: 8.5", L: 9". Similar to the previous lion but probably made in Staffordshire or in northeast England. The copper luster is most unusual. Price C. *John Howard; www.antiquepottery.co.uk*.

Figure 126.53. Lioness, to the left, with bocage with a snake in the branches. Probably attributable to Leather Leaf Group. H: 7.7". The fronds, the painting style, and the similarity to the following lioness suggest the attribution. Price C. *Newcastle-under-Lyme Museum*.

Figure 126.54. Lion and lioness, a pair, with bocages with a snake coiled in the branches of each. Attributed to Leather Leaf Group. H: 7.9". The curled bocage fronds with acorns and the painting of the base support the attribution. Price C. *John Howard; www.antiquepottery.co.uk*.

Figure 126.55. Lion to the right, with bocage with a snake coiled in the branches. Attributed to Leather Leaf Group. H: ~7.6". The bocage flowers are specific to the Group. Price C.

Figure 126.56. Lion and lioness, a pair, with bocages with a snake coiled in the branches of each. Attributed to Patriotic Group. H: ~8". The holly bocage fronds are specific to the Patriotic Group. Price C.

Figure 126.57. Pair of lions, each with a paw on a ball; with bocages. L: 6". Known only from these examples and desirable figures, despite the obvious bocage damage. Price C. *Image courtesy of The Potteries Museum & Art Gallery, Stoke-on-Trent, UK.*

Figure 126.58. Lion, to the right. L: ~6.5". An unusual lion. Made without bocage. Price C. *John Howard; www.antiquepottery.co.uk.*

Figure 126.59. Lion, to the right. H: 5.2". Probably from the same molds as the previous lion. Made without bocage. Price C. *Andrew Dando Antiques.*

Figure 126.60. Panther, to the left. L: ~7". Possibly the companion model to the previous lion model and perhaps from some of the same molds as the following leopard. Price B. *Andrew Dando Antiques.*

126.61. Leopard, to the left. L: ~7". Perhaps from the same figure molds as the previous panther. Price C.

Figure 126.62. Tiger, to the right; with bocage. Attributed to Dale. H: ~6". These twelve-petalled bocage flowers are strongly linked to Dale. The bright green base is also a common Dale feature. Price C. *John Howard; www.antiquepottery.co.uk.*

Figure 126.63. Lioness, to the right, with bocage. Attributed to Dale. H: ~6". The bocage is restored, but the distinctive twelve-petalled flowers on the base support the attribution. Price A.

Figure 126.64. Lion with a paw on a ball, to the left; with bocage. Attributed to Dale. H: ~6". Sprigs on the base (painted green) are thought to be specific to Dale. Bocage restored in the manner of Dale. Price A.

Figure 126.65. Lioness, to the right. Probably made by Dale. L: ~6". Made without bocage. Tooling on the base and the similarity to the following tiger support a Dale attribution. Price C. *John Howard; www.antiquepottery.co.uk.*

Figure 126.66. Tiger, to the right. Attributed to Dale. H: 6.5", L: 8". Bocage, leg, and tail lost. The floral sprigs on the base are specific to Dale. The rows of tooling on the base and the apple-green color are typical of Dale. Price B. *Stair Galleries.*

Figure 126.67. Tiger, to the right; with bocage. Attributed to Dale. H: ~7". The tooled depressions on the base, the bocage leaves and flowers, and the apple-green base are typical of Dale. Pairs with the following lion. Price C.

Figure 126.68. Lion with a paw on a ball, to the left; with bocage. Attributed to Dale. H: ~7". Companion to the previous tiger, with similar features supporting the attribution. Price C.

Figure 126.69. Lion with a paw on a ball, to the right; with bocage. Attributed to Patriotic Group. H: 5.3". The bocage flowers and base are specific to the Group. Much rarer than the next lions from the same pot bank and, unlike them, does not wear a harness. Price C.

Figure 126.70. Lion, to the right; with bocage. Attributed to Patriotic Group. H: ~5.5". More common than the previous lion. The lion wears a harness because this lion model also draws large chariots made by the same pot bank (Vol. 4, chap. 196). Price B.

Figure 126.71. Lion, to the right; with bocage. Attributed to Patriotic Group. H: ~5.5". Like the previous lion, but the base is painted differently. Companion to the following lion. Price B. *Collection of Michael J. Smith.*

Figure 126.72. Lion, to the left; with bocage. Attributed to Patriotic Group. H: 5.7". Companion to the previous lion. Again, this lion wears a harness because this figure pulls large chariots made by the same pot bank. Price B.

Figure 126.73. Lion, to the right; with bocage. Attributed to Patriotic Group. H: ~5.5", L: 4.8". From the same molds as previous Patriotic Group lions and similarly wears a harness. Companion to the following lion. Price B.

Figure 126.75. Pair of leopards; with bocages. H: 5.4". Attributed to Patriotic Group. The same bases and bocages are on Patriotic Group lions, dogs, horses, and sheep. Price C.

Figure 126.74. Lion to the left; with bocage. Attributed to Patriotic Group. H: ~5.5", L: 4.8". Companion to the previous lion and has the same distinctive Patriotic Group base and bocage. Price B.

Figure 126.76. Leopard, to the right; with bocage. Attributed to Patriotic Group. H: ~5.5". Patriotic Group leopards, like the lions, wear harnesses because they, too, pull chariots made by the same pot bank (Vol. 4, chap. 196). Price B.

Figure 126.77. Feline with a paw on a ball, to the right; with bocage. Attributed to Patriotic Group. H: 6". Price B. *Collection of Michael J. Smith.*

Figure 126.78. Lioness, to the right; with bocage. H: 4.8". Only traces of enamel paint remain on this figure. Of the same form as the following "Sherratt" lionesses but lacks "Sherratt" features. Price A. *Image courtesy of The Potteries Museum & Art Gallery, Stoke-on-Trent, UK.*

Figure 126.79. Lioness, to the right; with bocage. Attributed to "Sherratt." H: ~4.1". The floral sprigs applied to the base are specific to "Sherratt," and this bocage occurs on other "Sherratt" figures. Price B.

Figure 126.80. Lioness, to the right; with bocage. Attributed to "Sherratt." H: 3.9". Like the previous lioness but with a different "Sherratt" base and bocage. Price B. *Michael Goodacre.*

Figure 126.81. Leopard, to the right; with bocage. Attributed to "Sherratt." H: ~5.7". This base, usually with three flowers placed on it, occurs with many other "Sherratt" figures. Pairs with the following leopard. Price B. *Moore Collection.*

Figure 126.82. Leopard, to the left; with bocage. Attributed to "Sherratt." H: 5.7". Pairs with the previous leopard. Price B. *W. W. Warner Antiques.*

Figure 126.83. Leopard, to the left; with bocage. Attributed to "Sherratt." H: 4.5". Like the previous leopard but with a different "Sherratt" base and bocage. The floral sprigs applied to the base are exclusive to "Sherratt." Price B.

Figure 126.84. Leopard, to the left; with bocage. Attributed to "Sherratt." H: 7.8". Larger than previous "Sherratt" leopards and the only example of this scale recorded. The base and oak-leaf bocage with mayflowers are characteristic of this pot bank. Price C. *The William Herbert and Nancy Hunt Collection.*

Figure 126.85. Lioness, lion with owl, a pair, both with spill vases. Attributed to "Sherratt." H: ~5". Known from only these examples. The floral sprigs applied to the bases establish the attribution. Price D. *Photograph Courtesy of Sotheby's, Inc. © 2014.*

Figure 126.86. Pair of lions, each with a paw on a ball; with bocages. H: 5.7", L: 6". Price C. *Elinor Penna.*

Figure 126.87. Lion with a paw on the ball, to the right; with bocage. H: 5.8". Like the lion in the previous pair, but now red flower stalks are added to the bocage and the flowers integral to the base are picked out in red. Price B. *Collection of Michael J. Smith.*

Figure 126.88. Pair of lions, each with a paw on a ball; with bocages. H: 5.8". Like the previous pair of lions but with flowers on the bocages. Price C. *The William Herbert and Nancy Hunt Collection.*

Figure 126.89. Lion with a paw on a ball, to the right; with bocage. H: 6". Like the previous lion but with a bocage comprising hawthorn leaves. Price B. *Anthony James & Son.*

Figure 126.91. *LION*. Lion to the left; with bocage. Attributed to Daisy Group. H: 5.2". Usually Daisy Group flowers are painted red or pink. From the same molds as some of the following small lions. The enamels fired poorly but not unattractively. Price B. *Andrew Dando Antiques.*

Figure 126.90. Lion with a paw on a ball, to the left. H: ~5". A rare small feline on an unusual base. Price B. *Andrew Dando Antiques.*

Figure 126.92. *LION*, base of previous example. Dirt was trapped in the glaze during firing. *Andrew Dando Antiques.*

Figure 126.93. *LIONES*. Lioness with a paw on a ball, to the right; with bocage. H: 4.3". Striped like a tiger and pairs with the following lion. Price B. *W. W. Warner Antiques*.

Figure 126.94. *LION*. Lion with a paw on a ball, to the left; with bocage. H: 4.4". Striped (with later over painting) to pair with the previous lioness. Price B. *W. W. Warner Antiques*.

Figure 126.95. *LION*. Lion with a paw on a ball, to the left; with bocage. H: ~4.4". From the same molds as the previous lion, but the lion's tail is placed differently. The bocage is restored. Price A.

Figure 126.96. Lion, to the left; with bocage. Possibly made by Hall. H: ~4.4". Untitled and, like the following small Hall felines, has the paw extended to compensate for the lack of a ball. The bocage is largely restored in the manner of Hall. Price A.

Figure 126.97. Tiger, to the right; with bocage. Attributed to Hall. H: 4.5". The bocage flowers support the attribution. The end of the tiger's paw has been painted blue to simulate the ball that might normally be placed beneath it. Price B.

Figure 126.98. Leopard and tiger, a pair; with bocages. Attributed to Hall. H: 4.5". These bocage flowers only occur on figures that link to Hall, and the overall appearance of the bocage fronds is typical of Hall. Price C. *Collection of Michael J. Smith.*

Figure 126.99. Feline, to the left; with bocage. Probably made by Hall. H: ~4.5". The bocage flowers are like Hall's. The tiger is from the same figure molds as the Hall tiger in figure 126.98, with its paw again extended to compensate for the lack of a ball. Price B.

Figure 126.100. Tiger, to the left; with bocage. H: ~4". Price B.

Figure 126.101. Lion with a paw on a ball, to the left. H: ~3". Made without bocage. Price A.

Figure 126.102. Lion with a paw on a ball and on a tasseled cushion, to the left. H: 3". A regal lion, with the ball painted to simulate the globe. See figure 126.118 for similar lions crouching. Price B. *Jonathan Horne.*

Figure 126.103. Lion with a paw on a ball and on a tasseled cushion, to the left. H: 2.8", L: -3.2". This lion's human expression is particularly appealing. Dogs occur on similar cushions (figs. 120.49–51). Price B. *John Howard; www.antiquepottery.co.uk.*

Figure 126.104. Pair of small lions, each on a tasseled cushion with a paw on a ball. L: 3.3". See figure 126.95 for a similar lion before a bocage. Price B.

Figure 126.105. Lion at Heaton Hall, Manchester, made by John Bacon in the eighteenth century. This dog-like lion may have inspired the Wood & Caldwell/Enoch Wood lions in figures 126.106–110. *Richerman at the English language Wikipedia.*

Figure 126.107. Recumbent lions, a pair. Impressed "WOOD & CALDWELL". L: 5". Like the previous lion but painted differently. Price C. *Photograph Courtesy of Sotheby's, Inc. © 2014.*

Figure 126.106. Recumbent lion, to the right. Impressed "WOOD & CALDWELL". L: 5". Probably after John Bacon's lion at Heaton Hall. Similar lions were made into the Victorian era. Price B. *Andrew Dando Antiques.*

Figure 126.108. Recumbent lion, to the right. Probably made by Wood & Caldwell/Enoch Wood. L: 5". This lion could have been made during the Wood & Caldwell era or shortly thereafter. Companion to the following lion. Price A. *Andrew Dando Antiques.*

Figure 126.109. Recumbent lion, to the left. Probably made by Wood & Caldwell/Enoch Wood. L: 4.9". Companion to the previous lion. Price A. *Image courtesy of The Potteries Museum & Art Gallery, Stoke-on-Trent, UK.*

Figure 126.110. Recumbent lion, to the right; with bocage. Impressed "WALTON". H: 3.8". Companion to the following lion. Price B. *Collection of Michael J. Smith.*

Figure 126.111. Recumbent lion, to the left; with bocage. Impressed "WALTON". H: ~4.8". Companion to the previous lion. Price B.

Figure 126.112. Pair of recumbent leopards. L: 8.2". Such fine leopards are rare, and even single examples are much sought after. The right hand leopard has prey beneath its front right paw, but this model has been noted without this feature. Price F. *Nick Burton.*

Figure 126.113. Recumbent leopard, to the right. H: 2.6", L: 4.4". The base is decorated in under-glaze green, but the leopard's spots are enamel-painted. Price A. *Brighton and Hove Museums.*

Figure 126.114. Pair of recumbent lions. H: 5.3"; L: 7". A very unusual pair, known from only this example. Price D. *The William Herbert and Nancy Hunt Collection.*

Figure 126.115. Recumbent lion, to the left. L: 5". A fantastically expressive figure. Price B. *John Howard; www.antiquepottery.co.uk.*

Figure 126.116. Recumbent lion, to the left. L: 3.2". A relatively common feline constructed from simple molds. Price A.

Figure 126.117. Recumbent lion on a tasseled cushion, to the left. L: ~3.5". Price A. *Martyn Edgell Antiques Ltd.*

Figure 126.118. Assembled pair of crouching lions, each on a tasseled cushion. L: 3.8". A standing lion on a cushion is in the same style (fig. 126.102). Price A each. *The William Herbert and Nancy Hunt Collection (left).*

Figure 126.119. LIONES. Recumbent lioness, to the right; with bocage. L: 3.4". The small standing felines in figures 126.91–96 are on very similar bases. Price A.

Figure 126.120. Recumbent lion, to the left. H: 4.2". Price A. *Elinor Penna.*

Figure 126.121. Pair of prowling leopards. H: 2", L: 2.5". These and other similar leopards are after porcelain figures introduced by Derby circa 1765. Like most small exotic animals, they are rare and command a price premium. Made without bocages. Price C. *John Howard; www.antiquepottery.co.uk.*

Figure 126.122. Prowling leopard, to the left; with bocage. H: 2.7". Like the previous example but with bocage. Price B. *Image courtesy of The Potteries Museum & Art Gallery, Stoke-on-Trent, UK.*

Figure 126.123. Prowling leopard, to the left; with bocage. H: ~3". Like the previous leopard but with three-leaflet bocage fronds. Price B. *Andrew Dando Antiques.*

Figure 126.124. Recumbent leopard with cub; with spill vase and bocage. H: ~4.5". A similar pair is recorded. Price B.

Figure 126.125. Prowling leopard, to the left; with spill vase. H: ~4". Price B.

Figure 126.126. Prowling leopard, to the left. L: ~3.5". Price B. *Image courtesy of The Potteries Museum & Art Gallery, Stoke-on-Trent, UK.*

Figure 126.127. Prowling leopard, to the right. L: 4.7". The bocage is restored. Price A. *Brighton and Hove Museums.*

Figure 126.128. Prowling tiger, to the left. H: 3.6", W: ~4.4". Price C. *John Howard; www.antiquepottery.co.uk.*

Figure 126.129. Prowling leopard, to the left. L: 4.3". Like the previous tiger but painted to resemble a leopard. Price C. *Andrew Dando Antiques.*

Figure 126.130. *LIONESS* (title impressed on base). L: ~4.5". The reverse of the figure is flat. Decorated with both enamel and under-glaze colors. Price B. *John Howard; www.antiquepottery.co.uk.*

Figure 126.131. Lion and lioness, each with a cherub atop its back. A pair; with bocages. Attributed to Patriotic Group. H: 5"(L), 4.8"(R). The bocage flowers substantiate the attribution. Ralph Wood made a color-glazed lion and lioness, each with a cherub astride. This theme may be interpreted as love conquering all. Price C. *The William Herbert and Nancy Hunt Collection.*

Figure 126.132. Lioness with a cherub atop its back, to the left; with bocage. Attributed to Patriotic Group. H: ~5.5". The figures are from the same molds as the previous Patriotic Group lioness and cherub. Fern bocage fronds are consistent with the attribution. Price B.

Figure 126.133. Lion with a cherub atop its back, to the right; with bocage. Attributed to Patriotic Group. H: 5.8". The holly bocage is specific to the Patriotic Group. Price B. *The William Herbert and Nancy Hunt Collection.*

Figure 126.134. A pair of lions, each with a putto on its back. H: ~4". More naïve than previously illustrated pairs on this theme. Price B.

Figure 126.135. Lion attacking sheep; with spill vase. H: ~6.5". Price B.

Figure 126.136. Lion with a paw on a ball, to the right, with a cub, with a spill vase. H: ~5". Other animal subjects (figs. 123.7, 119.79–80, 131.94–95,) occur with similar distinctively shaped spill vases, as does figure 197.79 (Vol. 4). Price B.

Figure 126.137. Lion with a paw on a ball, to the right, with a fox, with a spill vase. H: ~5". From the same pot bank as the previous spill vase. Price B.

Figure 126.138. Recumbent lion, to the right, with a lamb, with a spill vase. H: 5.7". Price B. *The Bowes Museum, Barnard Castle.*

Figure 126.139. Tobacco jar with a lamb on the inner press and a lion surmounting the cover. H: 5.9". The lion and lamb reflect the Christian prophecy that "the lion shall lie down with the lamb." Price C. *John Howard; www.antiquepottery.co.uk*

Figure 126.140. Footed box with cover surmounted by a lion, its paw atop a ball. H: 7". Price D. *Doyle New York.*

Figure 126.141. Footed box with cover surmounted by a lion. H: 6.5". This lion model is normally found within performing bear groups. Price C. *John Howard; www.antiquepottery.co.uk.*

Figure 126.142. Watch stand with two vendors with baskets, with two lions atop. H: 8.9". Note the resemblance to figure 199.44 in Volume 4. On both, the underneath of the top shelf is painted. Price C. *Brighton and Hove Museums.*

Figure 126.143. Watch stand, previous example turned to show the painting beneath the top shelf. *Brighton and Hove Museums.*

Figure 126.144. Watch stand with a tyler mason to either side and two lions atop. H: 7.3". Note the resemblance to the previous watch stand and to figure 199.44 in Volume 4. The metal watch in place is original. Price C. *John Howard; www.antiquepottery.co.uk.*

Figure 126.145. Watch stand with a small recumbent lion. H: ~10.6". A similar watch stand impressed "FELL NEWCASTLE B" is recorded. Price C. *John Howard; www.antiquepottery.co.uk.*

Figure 126.146. Watch stand with a small recumbent lion atop. H: 9.6". Price B. *The William Herbert and Nancy Hunt Collection.*

Figure 126.147. Watch stand with a small recumbent lion atop. H: 8.1", L: 8.3". Price B. *The William Herbert and Nancy Hunt Collection.*

127. Mice

Only five earthenware mice are recorded, two of which are paired with cats. In both pairs, the mouse sits on a longer base than the cat, the extra length being necessary to accommodate the mouse's tail. In addition to the mice shown here, a mouse paired with a cat (like the cat in figure 116.21) has been documented.

Figure 127.1. Cat and mouse, a pair, both on rectangular bases. L: 2.4"(L), 2.7"(R). Price C.

Figure 127.2. Mouse. L: ~2.5". Price B. *John Howard; www.antiquepottery.co.uk.*

Figure 127.3. Mouse. L: 3". Price B.

128. Mythical Animals

In the early nineteenth century, there was pervasive belief in the existence of creatures that we now know to be mythical. Because photography had not yet been invented, it was difficult for the common man to distinguish fact from fantasy. Traveling menageries were to be invaluable in dispelling the illusions that centuries of folklore had built, and when mythical beasts failed to materialize in menagerie cages, there was a dawning awareness that they might not exist. In addition to the mythical creatures shown here, a small figure (height 2.3") with the head of a horse and the tail of a fish has been documented.

Figure 128.1. Mermaid. H: 9.6". A rare figure. Pairs with the following mermaid. Probably made circa 1822, when the display of a fake mermaid in London drew much attention. Price B.

Figure 128.2. Mermaid. H: 9.2". Pairs with the previous mermaid. Only three of these tall mermaids are recorded. Price B.

Figure 128.3. Recumbent mermaid. H: 3.3". Price B. ©*Victoria and Albert Museum, London.*

Figure 128.4. Vase with two sphinxes. H: ~8". Price A.

Figure 128.5. Vase with two sphinxes. H: 4.4". The base and the sphinxes are like those on the previous vase. Price A. *Image courtesy of The Potteries Museum & Art Gallery, Stoke-on-Trent, UK.*

129. Other Animals

Figure 129.1. Bear. H: 2.1". Rare. The bear's association with the sport of bear baiting may have made it an unpalatable adornment for refined homes. Price B. *Brighton and Hove Museums.*

Figure 129.3. Tortoise, serves as a flask. L: 5.6". Only this example is known. John Wood's order book for July 9, 1785, records the sale of "16 Tortoises & pairs." Price C. © *Victoria and Albert Museum, London.*

Figure 129.2. Hedgehog, serves as a crocus planter. L: 11.4". Price B. *Andrew Dando Antiques.*

Figure 129.4. Pig with spill vase. H: ~6". Pigs of this sort are associated with the Scottish potteries. Probably with both enamel and under-glaze decoration. Price C.

Figure 129.5. Pig with spill vase. H. 5.8". Made by one of the Scottish potteries and decorated with both enamel and under-glaze colors. Price C.

Figure 129.6. Dolphins on a vase. H: 7.7". The vase is formed identically on both sides, with each side having a dolphin down the center. A vase of the same form in the Laing Art Gallery (E.2436) is impressed "LEEDS POTTERY". Price A. *Elinor Penna.*

Figure 129.7. Watch stand with dolphins. H: 9". A very unusual watch stand, distinguished by both its form and decoration. Price C. *The William Herbert and Nancy Hunt Collection.*

Figure 129.8. Watch stand, previous example. Transfer print designs are on the front and sides of the base but not the back. *The William Herbert and Nancy Hunt Collection.*

Figure 129.9. Detail of the previous watch stand. A figure of Jupiter also has somewhat similar transfer prints on the base (Vol. 4, fig. 177.9). *The William Herbert and Nancy Hunt Collection.*

Figure 129.10. Figural pipe depicting a monkey. H: 3.8". Restored bowl. Price A. *Collection of Arnold and Barbara Berlin.*

Figure 129.12. Monkey. H: 2.7". Price B. *Andrew Dando Antiques.*

Figure 129.11. Figural pipe depicting a monkey. H: 4.6". Price B. *Elinor Penna.*

130. Rabbits and Hares

The pursuit of the hare was the focus of the sport of coursing, which was part of the fabric of British sporting life from Elizabethan times until its banning in 2004. The crafty hare was one of the select species that game law reserved for the exclusive hunting pleasure of wealthy landed gentry. Rabbits, on the other hand, were farmed for their skin and for food, and property law decreed that they belonged to the person on whose land they were located. Poaching hares or rabbits in violation of the law resulted in ruthless punishment that sometimes cost lives.

Figure 130.1. Pair of small rabbits. L: ~2.8". Very rare. Price C. *John Howard; www.antiquepottery.co.uk.*

Figure 130.2. Hare, running to the left; with bocage. Impressed "WALTON". H: 3.7", L: 4". A rare figure comprising part of a garniture that includes sportsmen, dogs, and birds (Vol. 2, figs. 84.66–67; Vol. 3, fig.120.32). Price B.

Figure 130.3. Recumbent rabbit. H: 2", L: 4". Price B. *Image courtesy of The Potteries Museum & Art Gallery, Stoke-on-Trent, UK.*

Figure 130.4. Recumbent rabbit. H: 1.6", L: 2". Price A. *John B. Watson.*

131. Sheep

Sheep with bemused expressions are perhaps the most common of Staffordshire figures, but their innate charm ensures their perennial popularity. It is fitting that Staffordshire potters paid tribute to the sheep for it was one of the most economically significant animals of its time. Thomas Bewick noted, "There is hardly any part of this animal that is not serviceable to man: of the fleece we make our cloaths; the skin produces leather, of which are made gloves, parchment, and covers for books; the entrails are formed into strings for fiddles and other musical instruments, likewise coverings for whips; its milk affords both butter and cheese; and its flesh is a delicate and wholesome food."[1]

In earlier centuries, the sheep had been a scraggly animal valued only for its pelt. After 1750, advances in animal husbandry transformed sheep into plump delights for the dinner table. As a result of changes in diet and breeding, sheep ballooned in size from an average weight of 23 pounds in 1700 to an astounding 80 pounds in 1828.[2] People must have looked at these bloated beasts in awe, remembering the scrawnier animals of their youth. Lots of people farmed sheep for a living, and potters turned out scores of sheep that adorned homes across England with pride.

Figure 131.1 Ram, to the right; with bocage. Impressed "HALL". H: 5.8". No other sheep is known with birds on its base. These bocage flowers are exclusive to Hall. Price B. *Eileen and Robert Carde.*

Figure 131.2. Ram, reverse of previous example showing "HALL" impressed in a small tablet. *Eileen and Robert Carde.*

Figure 131.3. Ram, to the right; with bocage. Impressed "HALL". H: 4.7". The large hindquarters are typical of Hall rams. Price A. *Michael Goodacre.*

Figure 131.4. Ewe with lamb, to the left; with bocage. Impressed "HALL". H: ~5". Only the bocage frond to the left of the ewe is original. Price A.

Figure 131.5. Ram and a ewe with a lamb, a pair; with bocages. Impressed "HALL". H: 5.5". The clusters of flowers on the bocages and bases are specific to Hall. Price B. *Bamfords Auctioneers and Valuers Ltd.*

Figure 131.6. Ewe with lamb, to the left; with bocage. Impressed "HALL". H: ~5.5". Like the ewe in the previous pair, but the bocage has carnations as well as the flower cluster that is specific to Hall. Price A.

Figure 131.7. Ram and a ewe with a lamb, a pair; with bocages. Impressed "HALL". H: ~5.8". The bocage flowers are the same carnations used by very many pot banks, but Hall favored painting them red and blue. Price B.

Figure 131.8. Ram and a ewe with a lamb, an assembled pair; with bocages. Impressed "HALL". H: ~5.8". Price A.

Figure 131.9. Ram and ewe each with a lamb, a pair; with bocages. Ewe impressed "HALL". Ram unmarked but attributed to Hall. H: ~5.8". Price A.

Figure 131.10. Ram, to the right; with bocage. Attributed to Dale. H: 5.8". The grape sprig and flowers establish the attribution. Dale sheep are quirky and, despite their similarity to Hall sheep, are readily recognizable. Price B.

Figure 131.11. Ram, to the right. Attributed to Dale. H: ~4.7". From the same molds as the previous ram. Only Dale and Tittensor used the twelve-petalled flowers that are on the base. Made without a bocage. Price A.

Figure 131.12. Ram to the right; with bocage. Attributed to Dale. H: ~5.8". The bocage is restored, but the floral sprigs on the base confirm the attribution. Price A.

Figure 131.13. Ram and ewe each with a lamb, a pair; with bocages. H: ~7.5". Impressed "WALTON". Walton sheep occur with much variation in the bocage flowers. Here both bocages have rounded flowers with six petals. Price B. *John Howard; www.antiquepottery.co.uk.*

Figure 131.14. Ram with lamb, to the right; with bocage. Marked "WALTON" in raised letters. H: 6.5". Each bocage flower has eight irregularly sized pointed petals. Walton sheep of this scale are only recorded with generic five-leaflet bocage fronds. They occur marked in either impressed or raised letters. Price B.

Figure 131.15. Ram and ewe each with a lamb, a pair; with bocages. Impressed "WALTON". H: 7.5". The ram's bocage flowers have six pointed petals; those on the ewe's bocage are very rounded with six petals. A true pair, despite this difference. Price B. *Andrew Dando Antiques.*

Figure 131.16. Ram with lamb, to the right, with bocage and spill vase. Impressed "WALTON". H: 7.3". The bocage flowers have four pointed petals. Companion to the following ewe. Price B.

Figure 131.17. Ewe with lamb, to the left, with bocage and spill vase. Impressed "WALTON". H: 6.8". Companion to the previous ram. The bocage flowers have six pointed petals. Price A. *Whitehall Antiques, Chapel Hill, North Carolina.*

Figure 131.18. Ram with lamb, to the right, with bocage and spill vase. Impressed "WALTON". H: 7". The bocage flowers have eight pointed petals and are of a type not seen on the previous Walton sheep. Price B. *John Howard; www.antiquepottery.co.uk.*

Figure 131.19. Ewe with lamb, to the left, with bocage and spill vase. Marked "WALTON". H: ~7". Black sheep are extraordinarily uncommon. This is the only marked example. Price B. © *National Trust/Geoff Lowsley; nationaltrust.org.uk.*

Figure 131.20. Ewe and ram, an assembled pair; with bocages. Impressed "WALTON". H: 4.9". Price A.

Figure 131.21. Ewe to the right; with bocage. Impressed "WALTON". H: ~4.9". Like the previous Walton ewe but decorated in a more typical Walton palette and having different bocage flowers. Price A.

Figure 131.22. Ewe and ram, a pair; with bocages. H: ~4.9". Like the previous Walton pair, but because these three-leaflet bocage fronds do not occur on marked Walton figures, an attribution is not possible. Price A.

Figure 131.23. A pair of sheep; with bocages. H: ~4.9". The sheep on the left has a restored bocage; minor restoration to the other bocage. Price A.

Figure 131.24. Ram, to the left; with bocage. H: 3.9". Price A. *Eileen and Robert Carde.*

Figure 131.25. Ram, reverse of previous ram. *Eileen and Robert Carde.*

Figure 131.26. Ewe, to the right; with spill vase and bocage. H: 5". The base is similar to that on the following ewe, and the bocage fronds and flowers are from the same molds. Price A. *The Bowes Museum, Barnard Castle.*

Figure 131.27. Ewe, to the left; with bocage. H: 5.6". Note the flowers (painted green) near the base of the bocage trunk. Probably from the same pot bank as the previous ewe. Price A. *The Bowes Museum, Barnard Castle.*

Figure 131.28. Ewe and ram each with a lamb, a pair; with bocages. Impressed "SALT". H: 6.5". Price B.

Figure 131.29. Ewe with a lamb, to the right; with bocage. H: ~6.3". Like the previous ram but unmarked and possibly made by any one of a number of potters. Price A. *Barbara Gair; www. castle-antiques.com.*

Figure 131.30. Ewe and ram each with a lamb, a pair; with bocages. H: 6.5". Like the Salt pair in figure 131.28, but the bocages have blue and pink carnations. Only pink and red carnations are recorded on marked Salt figures. Price B. *John Howard; www.antiquepottery.co.uk.*

Figure 131.31. Ram with a lamb, to the left; with bocage. H: 5.3". In the style of the Salt ram in figure 131.28 but possibly by another potter. Black sheep are known from a handful of examples. Price A. *Brighton and Hove Museums.*

Figure 131.32. Ewe and a ram with a lamb, a pair; with bocages. H: ~5". Price A.

Figure 131.33. Ram and ewe, a pair; with bocages. Attributed to Blue Group. H: ~6". The bocages, rather than the color of the bases, support the attribution. Price A.

Figure 131.34. Ram and ewe, a pair; with bocages. Attributed to Blue Group. H: ~6". Like the previous pair but in the green palette also used by the Blue Group. Price B.

Figure 131.35. Ram with a lamb, to the left; with bocage. Attributed to Blue Group. H: ~6.5". A different model ram to previous Blue Group examples and on a different base. Price A.

Figure 131.36. Ewe and ram each with a lamb, a pair; with bocages. Attributed to Blue Group. H: ~6.5". The ram is like that in figure 131.35 but with a different combination of bocage leaves and flowers. Price B. *John Howard; www.antiquepottery.co.uk.*

Figure 131.37. Ram and ewe, a pair; with bocages. Attributed to Blue Group. H: ~4.5". Smaller than the previous Blue Group pair but with the same bocage fronds. Price A.

Figure 131.38. Ram and ewe, a pair; with bocages. Attributed to Patriotic Group. H: 5.4". The bocages and bases support the attribution. Price B.

Figure 131.39. Ram and ewe each with a lamb, a pair; with bocages. Attributed to Patriotic Group. H: 5.5". Like the previous pair, but the bases (each now with a lamb) are different. The bocage flowers are specific to the Group. Price B.

Figure 131.40. Ewe, to the right; with bocage. Attributed to Patriotic Group. H: 2.8". Companion to the following ram. The flower on the bocage establishes the attribution. Price A. *Michael Goodacre.*

Figure 131.41. Ram, to the left; with bocage. Attributed to Patriotic Group. H: ~2.8". Companion to the previous ewe. Price A.

Figure 131.42. Sheep, to the right; with bocage. H: 2.4". Price A. *Michael Goodacre.*

Figure 131.43. Ewe to the left, with lamb; with bocage. H: 4.8". Price A. *Whitehall Antiques, Chapel Hill, North Carolina.*

Figure 131.44. Ewe with lamb, to the left; with bocage. Probably made by Enoch Wood. H: ~5.3". Each bocage frond has one leaflet atop four others. From the same molds as the following sheep, but the base is different. Price A. *Andrew Dando Antiques.*

Figure 131.45. Ewe with lamb, to the left; with bocage. Probably made by Enoch Wood. H ~5". Like the previous example but on a slightly different base. Price A.

Figure 131.46. Reverse of the bocage on the previous example. The fronds comprise one leaflet atop four in a typical Enoch Wood manner.

Figure 131.47. Ewe with lamb, to the left; with bocage. Probably made by Enoch Wood. H: 5". The base and seven-leaflet fern fronds match Enoch Wood shards. The initials painted on the ewe's back, "JH", were probably commissioned by the first purchaser. Price A. *Image courtesy of The Potteries Museum & Art Gallery, Stoke-on-Trent, UK.*

Figure 131.48. Reverse of the bocage on the previous example. These seven-leaflet fern fronds occur frequently on Enoch Wood figures, but other potters used them too. *Image courtesy of The Potteries Museum & Art Gallery, Stoke-on-Trent, UK.*

Figure 131.49. Ewe with lamb, to the left; with bocage. Probably made by Enoch Wood. H: 5.5". Like the previous sheep, but the bocage has five-leaflet fern fronds that match Enoch Wood shards. The initials "MO" are painted on the ewe's back. Price A. *Andrew Dando Antiques.*

Figure 131.50. Ewe, reverse of the previous example. Each bocage frond comprises five fern leaflets. *Andrew Dando Antiques.*

Figure 131.51. Ram, to the right; with bocage. Probably made by Enoch Wood. H: ~5.4". Companion to the previous ewe and has a bocage of the same form. Price A.

Figure 131.52. Ewe with suckling lamb, to the right; with bocage. Probably made by Enoch Wood. H: ~5.5". Pairs with the following ram. The pair is after earlier Derby figures. Price A. *Andrew Dando Antiques.*

Figure 131.53. Ram with lamb, to the left; with bocage. Probably made by Enoch Wood. H: ~5.6". Pairs with the previous ewe. After similar Derby porcelain models. Price A. *Andrew Dando Antiques.*

Figure 131.54. Ram with lamb, to the left; with bocage. Probably made by Enoch Wood. H: ~5.6". Like the previous ram, but each bocage frond comprises seven little fern leaflets, rather than one leaflet atop others. "BR" is painted on the ram's back. Price A.

Figure 131.55. Ram, to the left; with bocage. Probably made by Enoch Wood. H: 3". The smallest Enoch Wood-type sheep, with a typical bocage and base. Price A. *John Howard; www. antiquepottery.co.uk.*

Figure 131.56. Ewe, to the right; with bocage. Probably made by Enoch Wood. H: 3.2". The bocage, the thickly potted base, and the initials on the back are typical. Companion to the following ram. Price A. *Elinor Penna.*

Figure 131.57. Ram, to the left; with bocage. Probably made by Enoch Wood. H: ~3.4". Companion to the previous ewe and has initials painted on its back. The bocage is restored. Price A.

Figure 131.58. Ram with lamb, to the left; with bocage. Attributed to "Sherratt." H: ~5.3". The base and bocage are typical of "Sherratt." Sheep with black markings are uncommon. Price A.

Figure 131.59. Ewe and ram each with a lamb, a pair with bocages. Attributed to "Sherratt." H: ~5.3". The ram is like the previous ram but his lamb faces the other way. "Sherratt" also made this ram with a quite different head. Price A.

Figure 131.60. Ewe with lamb, to the right; with bocage. Attributed to "Sherratt." H: ~5.3". Like the previous ewe but with a different "Sherratt" bocage. This base with flowers added to the front is typical of "Sherratt." Price A.

Figure 131.61. Ewe, to the left; with bocage. Attributed to "Sherratt." H: 4.8". From different molds than previous "Sherratt" ewes. "Sherratt" frequently used this bocage with a turquoise palette. Characteristic sprigs are applied to the base. Price A. *Andrew Dando Antiques.*

Figure 131.62. Ram, to the right; with bocage. Attributed to "Sherratt." H: ~5.5". Different from previous "Sherratt" rams and faces in the opposite direction. Pairs with the following ewe. Price A.

Figure 131.63. Ewe with lamb, to the left; with bocage. Attributed to "Sherratt." H: ~5.5". Pairs with the previous ram and, like it, has characteristic floral sprigs on the base. The flowers on the sprigs and bocage are painted blue and yellow, a combination not normally seen on "Sherratt" flowers. Price A.

Figure 131.64. Ewe with lamb, to the left; with bocage. Attributed to "Sherratt." H: ~5.5". Like the previous ewe but with hawthorn bocage fronds (with restoration to extremities). This bocage form is only rarely encountered on "Sherratt" figures. Price A.

Figure 131.65. Ram, to the right; with bocage. H: ~5.5". The flower clusters and oak-leaf bocage fronds are suggestive of "Sherratt." Price A.

Figure 131.66. Ram, to the right; with bocage. H: ~5.5". Like the previous ram but with a different base, bocage fronds, and flower clusters, and from a different pot bank. An unclassified group of figures has these flower clusters. Figure 119.43 has the same combination of bocage fronds and flower clusters. Price A.

Figure 131.67. Ram, to the right; with bocage. H: ~5.5". Like the previous ram, with the base and flower clusters formed similarly. The bocage fronds are different, but both figures originate from the same pot bank. Price A.

Figure 131.68. Ewe and ram each with a lamb, a pair; with bocages. Attributed to Daisy Group. H" ~6". Price B. *John Howard; www.antiquepottery.co.uk.*

Figure 131.69. Ewe, to the right; with bocage. Attributed to Leather Leaf Group. H: ~5". The bocage flowers are specific to the Group, and the distinctive painting of the base is typical. Price A.

Figure 131.70. Ewe with lamb, to the left; with bocage. Attributed to Ralph Wood. H: ~6". Note the ewe's black face. The bocage (with some restoration) and the colors on the base support the attribution. Price A.

Figure 131.71. Ram with lamb, to the left. Impressed "SELMAN". H: ~6". The floral sprigs on the base are only otherwise recorded on Dale examples and seem to be of a comparable size. Price A. *Michael Goodacre.*

Figure 131.72. The "SELMAN" mark on the reverse of the previous ram. This name is associated with J. & W. Selman, toy makers, circa 1860, but this ram appears to be pre-Victorian. *Michael Goodacre.*

Figure 131.73. Ram, to the left; with bocage. H: 9.3". This very large ram stands on an unusual base and is the largest sheep recorded. Known from only this example. Price B. *The William Herbert and Nancy Hunt Collection.*

Figure 131.74. Ewe with lamb, to the right; with bocage. Attributed to Tunstall Group. H: ~5". The two lower left bocage fronds are original and are typical of the Group. Price A.

Figure 131.75. Ewe with lamb, to the right; with bocage. Attributed to Tunstall Group. H: ~5". Like the previous ewe but with different bocage fronds and characteristic flowers. Companion to the following ram. Price A.

Figure 131.76. Ram with lamb, to the left; with bocage. Attributed to Tunstall Group. H: ~5". Companion to the previous ewe. Price A.

Figure 131.77. Ewe with lamb, to the left; with bocage. Attributed to Big Blossom Group. H: ~5". Price A.

Figure 131.78. Ram with lamb, to the right; with bocage. H: ~6". Price A.

Figure 131.79. Ewe with lamb, to the right; with bocage. Attributed to Box Title Group. H: ~5.2". Some bocage restoration. Price A.

Figure 131.80. Ewe and ram each with a lamb, a pair; with bocages. H: ~5". The bocage fronds are restored. The flowers below the fronds are original. Price A.

Figure 131.81. Ewe with lamb, to the right; with bocage. H: ~5.6". An unusual bocage with the flowers on the branches. Companion to the following ram. Price A.

Figure 131.82. Ram with lamb, to the left; with bocage. H: ~5.6". The bocage fronds are restored, but the flowers are original. Companion to the previous ewe. Price A.

Figure 131.83. Ram, to the right; with bocage. H: ~5". Price A.

Figure 131.84. Ram with lamb, to the left; with bocage. H: ~5". Price A.

Figure 131.85. Ram, to the right; with bocage. H: ~4.5". Price A.

Figure 131.86. Reverse of bocage on previous example. This bocage occurs on other figures apparently from the same pot bank (Vol. 1, figs. 26.64, 28.43; Vol. 2, figs. 85.19, 108.37; and figs. 119.175, 131.179).

Figure 131.87. Ewe with lamb, to the left; with bocage. H: ~4.6". The lamb and ewe have remarkably similar expressions. Price A.

Figure 131-088. Ram, to the left. H: ~4". Made without bocage. The central stump sits under the ram and does not touch its back. Price A. *Andrew Dando Antiques.*

Figure 131.89. Ram, to the left; with bocage. H: ~6.5". The same model as the following ram. An unusual base with a floral design integral to the "ramp" under the ram's belly. Price A. *Andrew Dando Antiques.*

Figure 131.90. A pair of rams, one with a lamb, both with spill vases and bocages. H: 5". An unusual pair. Price B. *John Howard; www.antiquepottery.co.uk.*

Figure 131.91. Ram with lamb, to the right; with spill vase and bocage. H: ~5.7". Price A. *Barbara Gair; www.castle-antiques.com.*

Figure 131.92. Ram and ewe each with a lamb, a pair; with spill vases and bocages. H: ~6". These three-leaflet bocage fronds occur on an unclassified group of figures from the same pot bank. Price B.

Figure 131.93. Ram with a lamb, to the right; with a spill vase and bocage. H: 6". Like the ram in the previous pair, but the lamb is larger and, unusually, is painted black. The bocage again has three-leaflet bocage fronds. Price A. *Nick Burton.*

Figure 131.94. Ram with lamb, to the right; with spill vase and bocage. H: ~5.4". Other spill vases of this form (figs. 119.79–80, 123.7, 126.136–137, and Vol. 4, fig. 197.79) are probably from the same pot bank. Companion to the following ewe. Price A.

Figure 131.95. Ewe with lamb, to the left; with spill vase and bocage. H: ~5.4". Companion to the previous ram. Price A. *www.madelena.com.*

Figure 131.96. Ram, to the right; with spill vase and bocage. H: ~5". Price A.

Figure 131.97. Ewe, to the left; with spill vase and bocage. H: ~5". Bocage restored. Price A.

Figure 131.98. Ram with lamb, to the right; with spill vase. H: ~6.7". Price A.

Figure 131.99. Ram with lamb, to the right; with bocage and spill vase. Attributed to Patriotic Group. H: 5.6". Probable loss of bocage to left of spill vase. Price A. *Michael Goodacre.*

Figure 131.100. Ewe with lamb, to the left; with spill vase and bocage. Attributed to Leaf Mat Group. H: 4.4". A companion ram is documented. Price B. *John Howard; www.antiquepottery.co.uk.*

Figure 131.101. Reverse of the previous ewe showing the Leaf Mat bocage fronds. *John Howard; www.antiquepottery.co.uk.*

Figure 131.102. Ram and ewe, a pair. H: 2.8". An unusual pair. Price B. *John Howard; www.antiquepottery.co.uk.*

Figure 131.103. Ewe and ram, a pair; with bocages. Attributed to Starred Anthemion Group. H: 4.2". Price A.

Figure 131.104. Ram, to the left; with bocage. Attributed to Starred Anthemion Group. H: ~4.2". Like the previous ram but the base is decorated differently. Price A.

Figure 131.105. Ewe, to the right; with bocage. Attributed to Dudson. H: ~3.5". The bocage and partial x-sprigs on the base support the attribution. Price A.

Figure 131.106. Ewe, to the right; with bocage. H: ~3.5". The bocage comprises three-leaflet fronds. Price A.

Figure 131.107. Ewe, to the right; with bocage. Impressed "SALT". H: ~3.5". The bocage has hawthorn leaves rather than the five-leaflet fronds found on most Salt figures. Companion to the following ram. Price A. *Andrew Dando Antiques.*

Figure 131.108. Ram, to the left; with bocage. Impressed "SALT". H: ~3.5". Companion to the previous ewe. Price A.

Figure 131.109. Ram, to the left; with bocage. Attributed to Salt. H: 3.5". Like the previous ram but unmarked. The figure, the base, and the bocage fronds have been formed from the same molds as used for the previous ram. Price A. *Elinor Penna.*

Figure 131.110. Sheep, to the right; with bocage. H: ~3.5". The bocage has oak leaves and clusters of six-pointed flowers. Price A.

Figure 131.111. Ram, to the left; with bocage. H: ~3.5". With anthemion bocage leaves with six-petalled flowers. Price A.

Figure 131.112. Ram, to the left; with bocage. H: ~3.5". Price A.

Figure 131.113. Ram, to the left; with bocage. H: ~3.8". Bocage largely restored. Price A.

Figure 131.114. Ewe, to the right; with bocage. H: ~3.2". Price A.

Figure 131.115. Ram, to the left, bocage lost. H: ~3.5". Price A.

Figure 131.116. Pair of sheep; with bocages. H: ~2.7". Price A.

Figure 131.117. Ewe, to the right; with bocage. Attributed to Leaf Mat Group. H: ~4". Price A.

Figure 131.118. Ram, to the left; with bocage. Attributed to Leaf Mat Group. H: ~4". Price A.

Figure 131.119. Ram, to the right; with bocage. Attributed to Leaf Mat Group. H: ~4". Companion to the following ewe. Price A.

Figure 131.120. Ewe, to the left; with bocage. Attributed to Leaf Mat Group. H: ~4". Companion to the previous ram. Price A.

Figure 131.121. Ewe, to the left; with bocage. H: 4.3". This rounded bocage is unlike previous Leaf Mat Group examples and has flowers integral to the design. Price A. *W. W. Warner Antiques.*

Figure 131.122. Ewe, to the right; with bocage. H: ~3.4". Price A.

Figure 131.123. Sheep, to the right; with bocage. H: 3.1". Possibly made by "Sherratt." The bocage, the sheep, and the base suggest the attribution. Price A.

Figure 131.124. Sheep, to the right; with bocage. H: 3.6". Probably made by "Sherratt". "Sherratt" used a base with integral sheep for figures of musicians; the impressed design on the base is like that on other "Sherratt" bases; and the bocage is not inconsistent with attribution. Price A.

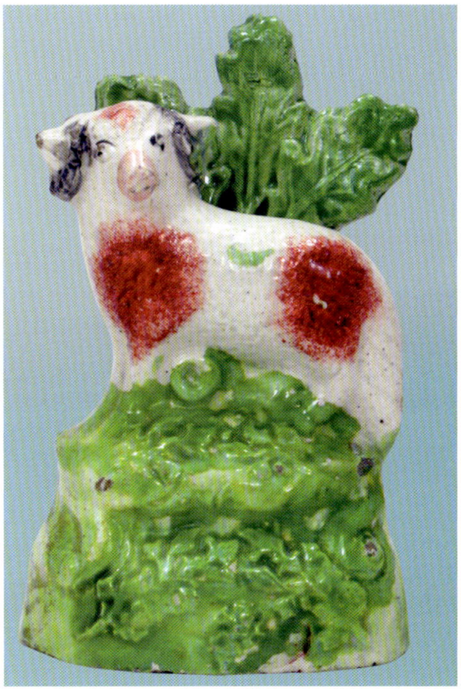

Figure 131.125. Ram, to the left; with bocage. H: ~3.6". Possibly made by "Sherratt." The impressed design on the base occurs on the bases of other small "Sherratt" figures. The bocage is restored. Price A.

Figure 131.126. Ram, to the right; with bocage. H: 4.7". Price A. *Andrew Dando Antiques.*

Figure 131.127. A pair of sheep; with bocages. H: 3.5". The bocages are flat on the back. Price A. *Peter Flemans.*

Figure 131.128. Pair of rams, one standing and the other seated; with bocages. H: ~4". Price A.

Figure 131.129. Pair of sheep; with bocages. H: 4". Price A.

Figure 131.130. Pair of sheep, reverse of previous pair showing their simple bocages. The size difference may be due to different rates of shrinkage in firing.

Figure 131.131. Sheep, to the left. H: 3.9". Probably made in Scotland. Made without bocage. Price A. *Andrew Dando Antiques.*

Figure 131.132. Pair of recumbent sheep; with bocages. Probably made by Enoch Wood. H: ~4". The bocage fronds (one leaflet atop four others) and flowers are typical of Enoch Wood. Price A.

Figure 131.133. Recumbent ewe, to the right; with bocage. Probably made by Enoch Wood. H: ~4". Like the previous ewe, but the bocage fronds now comprise seven tiny fern leaflets. The first owner's initials, "MH", are painted on the ewe's back. Companion to the following ram. Price A.

Figure 131.134. Recumbent ram, to the left; with bocage. Probably made by Enoch Wood. H: 4". A companion to the previous ewe, having the same bocage fronds. The initials "IM" are painted on the ram's back. Price A. *Martyn Edgell Antiques Ltd.*

Figure 131.135. Recumbent ram, to the right; with bocage. H: 4". In the style of Enoch Wood. Similar bocage fronds (each with five fern leaflets) occasionally occur on Enoch Wood figures (fig. 131.49). Price A. *Andrew Dando Antiques.*

Figure 131.136. Recumbent sheep, to the right; with bocage. H: ~3.8". Pairs with the following sheep. Price A.

Figure 131.137. Recumbent sheep, to the left; with bocage. H: 3.8". Pairs with the previous sheep. Price A.

Figure 131.138. Recumbent ram, to the right; with bocage. H: 4". Companion to the following ewe. Price A. Bernard Trower.

Figure 131.139. Recumbent ewe, to the left; with bocage. H: ~4". Companion to the previous ram. Price A.

Figure 131.140. Recumbent ewe, to the left; with bocage. H: 4". Like figure 131.39 but with a different bocage. Companion to the following ram. Price A.

Figure 131.141. Recumbent ram, to the right; with bocage. H: ~4". Like figure 131.38 but with a different bocage. Companion to the ewe in figure 131.40. Price A.

Figure 131.142. Recumbent ram, to the right; with bocage. H: 4". Companion to the following ewe and, like it, in the style of Salt. Price A.

Figure 131.143. Recumbent ewe, to the left; with bocage. H: ~4". Companion to the previous ram. Both have carnations on their bocages. Price A.

Figure 131.144. Recumbent ewe, to the left; with bocage. Attributed to Hall. H: ~4". The flowers are characteristic of Hall. Price A.

Figure 131.145. A pair of recumbent sheep; with bocages. H: ~4.5". Unlike most recumbent ewe-ram pairings, neither of these sheep has horns. Price A.

Figure 131.146. Recumbent ram, to the left; with bocage. H: ~4". Price A.

Figure 131.147. Recumbent sheep, to the left; with bocage. Attributed to Patriotic Group. H: ~4". A less common Patriotic Group frond form with a characteristic flower. Price A. *John Howard; www.antiquepottery.co.uk.*

Figure 131.148. Recumbent sheep, to the right; with bocage. H: 3.5". The bocage comprises cilantro leaves. Price A.

Figure 131.149. Recumbent ram, to the left; with bocage. Attributed to Tunstall Group. H: ~4". Price A.

Figure 131.150. Pair of recumbent sheep; with bocages. Attributed to Tunstall Group. H: ~4". Price A.

Figure 131.151. Recumbent ewe with lamb, to the right; with bocage. Attributed to "Sherratt." H: ~4.5". The bocage is characteristic of "Sherratt," and this pot bank frequently placed three small flowers across the fronts of bases. Price A.

Figure 131.152. Recumbent ewe with lamb, to the right; with bocage. Attributed to "Sherratt." H: ~4.5". Like the previous figure but unusual in that the sheep have black patches. Price A.

Figure 131.153. Recumbent ewe with lamb, to the right; with bocage. Attributed to "Sherratt." H: ~4.3". Like previous "Sherratt" sheep but with a quite different yet typical "Sherratt" bocage. Price A.

Figure 131.154. Recumbent ewe with lamb, to the right; with bocage. Attributed to "Sherratt." H: ~4.3". Like the previous ewe but with different bocage flowers. The small sheep may be positioned facing either way on such groups. Companion to the following ram. Price A.

Figure 131.155. Recumbent ram with lamb, to the left; with bocage. Attributed to "Sherratt." H: ~4.3". Companion to the previous ewe. Price A.

Figure 131.156. Recumbent ram with lamb, to the left; with bocage. Attributed to "Sherratt." H: 4.7". Like the previous ram but with less common double-anthemion bocage fronds. Price A.

Figure 131.157. Pair of recumbent sheep, with bocages, with birds in the branches. H" ~7.5". An unusual pair. Price A.

Figure 131.158. Recumbent ewe, to the left; with bocage. Attributed to Dudson. H: ~4.5". The bocage supports the attribution, and the base is very suggestive of Dudson. Price A.

Figure 131.159. Recumbent ram, to the right; with bocage. Possibly made by Dudson. H: ~5.5". The bocage is closely similar to Dudson bocages. Perhaps a companion figure to the previous Dudson ewe. Price A.

Figure 131.160. Pair of recumbent sheep; with bocages. Possibly made by Dudson. H: ~4.5". Black sheep are very unusual. The ewe (like the Dudson ewe in fig. 131. 58) has a restored bocage. Price B.

Figure 131.161. Recumbent sheep, to the left; with bocage. H: ~4". This sheep's coat is particularly well defined. Price A.

Figure 131.162. Recumbent sheep, to the left; with bocage. H: ~4". Price A.

Figure 131.163. Pair of recumbent sheep; with bocages. Impressed "SALT". H: ~5.5". Price B.

Figure 131.164. Recumbent sheep, to the right; with bocage. Probably made by Hall. H: ~5.2". The red and blue flowers, the enamels, and the standard of potting are very suggestive of Hall. Like the previous Salt ewe, and Hall's figures are sometimes copies of Salt's. Price A.

Figure 131.165. Recumbent ram, to the left; with bocage. H: ~5.9". Price A.

Figure 131.166. Pair of recumbent sheep; with bocages. Attributed to Patriotic Group. H: 4.7". The bocage flowers are specific to the Group. Price B.

Figure 131.167. Recumbent ram, to the right; with bocage. H: ~4". Price A.

Figure 131.168. Recumbent ram, to the right; with bocage. H: ~4". An unusual model and bocage. Price A.

Figure 131.169. Recumbent ram, reverse of previous figure.

Figure 131.170. Recumbent sheep, to the right; with bocage. H: ~3.5". Price A.

Figure 131.171. Recumbent ram, to the left. H: 2". Price A. *Michael Goodacre.*

Figure 131.172. Recumbent ram, to the right; with bocage. H: 2.8". The bocage, including the trunk, is formed separately from the figure and is flat and unpainted on the back. Price A.

Figure 131.173. Recumbent sheep to the left; with bocage. H: ~3". A most unusual bocage. Price A. *Andrew Dando Antiques.*

Figure 131.174. Recumbent sheep, reverse of previous sheep. This bocage (with some restoration) is otherwise unrecorded. *Andrew Dando Antiques.*

Figure 131.175. Pair of recumbent sheep; with bocages. H: 2.8". Price A. *Eileen and Robert Carde.*

Figure 131.176. Pair of recumbent sheep, reverse of previous pair. *Eileen and Robert Carde.*

Figure 131.177. Recumbent sheep, to the right; with bocage. Impressed "SALT". H: ~2". Acorns (painted green) are integral to the bocage leaves. In the same style as small Salt cows (fig. 118.87) and deer (fig. 119.173). Price A.

Figure 131.178. Pair of recumbent sheep; with bocages. Probably made by Salt. H: ~2". The ewe closely resembles the previous ewe and has identically formed bocage leaves (with acorns), so attribution to Salt seems reasonable. Price A.

Figure 131.179. Pair of recumbent sheep; with bocages. H: ~2.3". Stylistically similar to the previous pair but from different molds. This bocage occurs on other figures apparently from the same pot bank (Vol. 1, figs. 26.64, 28.43; Vol. 2, figs. 85.19, 108.37; and figs. 119.175, 131.85). Price A.

Figure 131.180. Pair of recumbent sheep; with bocages. Attributed to "Sherratt." H: ~2.8". The bocages and the leafy design integral to the bases are typical of "Sherratt." Price A.

Figure 131.181. Pair of recumbent sheep; with bocages. Attributed to "Sherratt." H: 2.8". With better enamels than the previous pair, but the pattern on the bases is less well defined. Price A.

Figure 131.182. Pair of recumbent sheep. Attributed to "Sherratt." H: 2.2". Like the previous two pairs and with the same pattern on the bases but made without bocages. Price A. *Andrew Dando Antiques.*

Figure 131.183. Five recumbent sheep; with bocage. Attributed to "Sherratt." H: ~4". Price A.

Figure 131.184. Three recumbent sheep and a dog; with bocage. H: ~4.5". Price A.

Figure 131.185. Four recumbent sheep and a dog; with bocage. H: ~4.5". On the same base and with the same bocage fronds as the previous and following examples and, like them, very much in the Walton style. Price A.

Figure 131.186. Five recumbent sheep; with bocage. H: ~4.5". Like the previous two examples but with a different assemblage of animals. Price A.

Figure 131.187. Four sheep, a goat, and a dog; with bocage. H: 5.7". In the Walton style, but these three-leaflet bocage fronds do not occur on marked Walton figures. Price A. *Elinor Penna.*

Figure 131.188. Four sheep, a goat, and a dog; with bocage. H: 5.7". Like the previous example but painted differently, and the goat is now on the left of the base. Price A.

Figure 131.189. Five recumbent sheep; with bocage. Attributed to Starred Anthemion Group. H: 6.3". Price A.

Figure 131.190. Recumbent sheep and goat; with bocage. Attributed to Starred Anthemion Group. H: ~4". Price A. *The Bowes Museum, Barnard Castle.*

Figure 131.191. Recumbent sheep and recumbent goat, a pair, each with a spill vase. H: 3.1". Price A.

Figure 131.92. Ram and ewe each with a lamb, a pair; with spill vases and bocages. H: ~6". These three-leaflet bocage fronds occur on an unclassified group of figures from the same pot bank. Price B.

Figure 131.93. Ram with a lamb, to the right; with a spill vase and bocage. H: 6". Like the ram in the previous pair, but the lamb is larger and, unusually, is painted black. The bocage again has three-leaflet bocage fronds. Price A. *Nick Burton.*

Figure 131.194. Two recumbent sheep and a bird; with spill vase. H: 3.7". Also recorded with a differently shaped bird. Price A. *Peter Flemans.*

Figure 131.195. Three recumbent sheep; with spill vase. H: ~4". Price A.

Figure 131.196. Three sheep and a goat; with spill vase. Probably made by Walton. H: ~4.7". Unmarked but very like the following marked Walton example. Price A.

Figure 131.197. Three sheep and a goat; with spill vase. Impressed "WALTON". H: 4.7". The mark is impressed beneath. Price A.

Figure 131.198. Three recumbent sheep and a dog; with spill vase. Impressed "WALTON". H: 4.7". The mark is impressed beneath. Price A.

Figure 131.199. Two recumbent sheep, a goat, and a dog; with spill vase. Impressed "WALTON". H: 4.7". The mark is impressed beneath. Price A.

Figure 131.200. Two sheep, a goat, and a dog; with spill vase. Impressed "WALTON". H: 4.7". The mark is impressed beneath. Very like the previous example, but the goat is placed and painted differently. Price A. *John Howard; www.antiquepottery.co.uk.*

Figure 131.201. Five recumbent sheep; with spill vase. H: ~4". Similar groups occur on this base with a bocage rather than a spill vase. Price A.

Figure 131.202.Three recumbent sheep; with spill vase. Attributed to Enoch Wood/Wood & Caldwell. H: 5". The large four-petalled flowers on the base support the attribution. Price A.

Figure 131.203. Three recumbent sheep; with spill vase. Attributed to Enoch Wood/Wood & Caldwell. H: 6". Flowers exclusive to Enoch Wood/Wood & Caldwell are generously applied to both the base and the spill vase. Price A.

Figure 131.204. Three recumbent sheep; with spill vase. Attributed to Enoch Wood/Wood & Caldwell. H: 6.2". Like previous examples but decorated with restraint. Price A. *Elinor Penna.*

Figure 131.205. Three recumbent sheep; with spill vase. Attributed to Enoch Wood/Wood & Caldwell. H: 6.3". Of the same form as the previous examples and with four-petalled flowers on the base and trunk that are specific to this pot bank. Price A. *Elinor Penna.*

Figure 131.206. Three recumbent sheep; with spill vase. Attributed to Enoch Wood/Wood & Caldwell. H: 6.2". Like previous examples and having flowers in the style of the Wood manufactory. Price A. *Elinor Penna.*

Figure 131.207. Three sheep; with spill vase. Attributed to Enoch Wood/Wood & Caldwell. H: 8.5". The base and the vase differ from those on previous examples from this pot bank, and two of the sheep are now standing. Price A. *Andrew Dando Antiques.*

Figure 131.208. Four sheep; with spill vase. Attributed to Enoch Wood/Wood & Caldwell. H: ~8.5". With the same base and vase as the previous and following examples. All three examples have flowers on the bases that are typical of this pot bank. Price A.

Figure 131.209. Four sheep and a goat; with spill vase. Attributed to Enoch Wood/Wood & Caldwell. H: 9.2". Price A. *Elinor Penna.*

Figure 131.210. Three sheep, a goat, and a deer; with spill vase. Attributed to Enoch Wood/Wood & Caldwell. H: 9.7". Price A. *Collection of Michael J. Smith.*

Figure 131.211. Two sheep and two birds; with spill vase. H: ~6". Price A.

Figure 131.212. Four sheep and a dog; with spill vase. Attributed to Patriotic Group. H: 6.5". The flower on the base is characteristic of Patriotic Group. This base and vase occur on other Patriotic Group examples and appear to be specific to it. Price B. *Saffron Walden Museum.*

Figure 131.213. Two sheep and a dog; with spill vase. H: 4.7". From the same pot bank as the following two examples. Price B.

Figure 131.214. Four sheep and a dog; with spill vase. H: ~4.7". Price B.

Figure 131.215. Four sheep; with spill vase. H: ~4.7". Like the previous two examples but with a different arrangement of small animals. Price B.

Figure 131.216. Three sheep; with spill vase. H: 7.8". Price B. *John Howard; www.antiquepottery.co.uk.*

Figure 131.217. Four sheep; with bocage. H: ~7.5". The large sheep and the base appear to be from the same molds as used in the previous example. Price B.

Figure 131.218. Six sheep with spill vase; with bocage to either side. H: ~6.5". Price B.

Figure 131.219. Three piece garniture, with sheep and goats before the spill vases. H: 7.6". Price A. *Woolley and Wallis Salisbury Salerooms Ltd.*

Figure 131.220. Flock of sheep and a dog lying before a spill vase, a large snake wound around it. H: ~9". Similar spill vase groups include a shepherd (Vol. 1, figs. 27.164–5). Price C. *John Howard; www.antiquepottery.co.uk.*

Figure 131.221. Sheep and goat with spill vase. Probably made by Dale. H: 7.8"; L: 9". Similar Dale spill vase groups include a shepherd (Vol. 1, figs. 27.166–168). Price B. *John Howard; www.antiquepottery.co.uk.*

Figure 131.222. Sheep spill vase. Attributed to Enoch Wood/Wood & Caldwell. L: 16.2". The small vases to either side of the central spill can be lifted off the base. See figure 119.5 for a similar spill vase with deer. Price B. *The William Herbert and Nancy Hunt Collection.*

132. Squirrels

The common grey squirrel was only introduced into England in Victorian times. The red squirrel, on the other hand, is native to the United Kingdom and is featured in early earthenware figures.

Figure 132.1. Squirrel; with bocage. H: ~5". The unusual bocage is recorded only on this rare squirrel and on the following pair. Price B. *John Howard; www.antiquepottery.co.uk.*

Figure 132.2. Base of previous example. *John Howard; www.antiquepottery.co.uk.*

Figure 132.3. Squirrels, a pair; with bocages. H: 4". Like the previous squirrel but on different bases. No other pair of squirrels is recorded. Price C. *John Howard; www.antiquepottery.co.uk.*

Figure 132.4. Squirrel. H: 3.5". The most common form of squirrel. Derby made a very similar squirrel model from circa 1780. Price B.

Figure 132.5. Squirrel. H: 3.3". Like the previous squirrel but on a different base. Price B. *Collection of Michael J. Smith.*

Figure 132.6. Squirrel. H: 3.8". Price A.

Figure 132.7. Squirrel. H: 3.3". Price A.

Figure 132.8. Squirrel. H: 3.3". Like the previous squirrel but painted differently. Price A. *Elinor Penna.*

133. Dandies

The years 1810 to 1830 brought to English fashion dandy gentlemen, who preened as never before. Appropriate attire for a dandy included a coat that fitted snugly at his waist (the waist was cinched with a corset, if necessary), a white shirt with a high collar, and a cravat that was knotted with the utmost precision. Because pockets could not disturb fit, dandies carried reticules for their necessary objects, and some earthenware dandies clutch such small handbags. Dandy ladies, sometimes called dandizettes, never reached the fashionable heights of their male counterparts, but they raised hemlines to expose their ankles for the first time and wore particularly large bonnets. Dandy attire and demeanor invited ridicule, and colorful contemporary engravings—notably George Cruikshank's Monstrosities series—poked fun at fashion's absurdities.

Today, dandy figure groups ooze personality and are popular at all price levels. Although some of the groups utilize closely similar molds, slight differences in placement or painting impart unique characteristics that allow each group to exude its own personality. Many dandy couples partner with similar groups arranged with the dandy and dandizette in switched positions. Possibly these groups were originally available for purchase as pairs.

Figure 133.1. Dandy and dandizette; with bocage. Attributed to "Sherratt." H: 9.4". This and its companion in the next example are the largest dandy groups. Both have "Sherratt" bocages and characteristic floral sprigs applied to their bases. Price D.

Figure 133.2. Dandy and dandizette; with bocage. Attributed to "Sherratt." H: ~9.4". Companion to the previous example. Both use the striking "Sherratt" turquoise palette. Price D.

Figure 133.3. Dandy and dandizette, a pair. Attributed to "Sherratt." H: 8.5". From the same molds used for the figures in the previous group. Typical "Sherratt" sprigs are applied to the bases. Price D. *Brighton and Hove Museums.*

Figure 133.4. Dandy and dandizette, reverse of the previous pair, made without bocages. *Brighton and Hove Museums.*

Figure 133.5. Dandizette. Attributed to "Sherratt." H: ~8.5". "Sherratt" sprigs are applied to the base. From the same molds as the dandizette in figure 133.1. Price B.

Figure 133.6. Dandy and dandizette; with spill vase. Attributed to "Sherratt." H: 8.7". Although smaller, the dandies pose like the couples in figures 133.2–3. The feathered base is specific to "Sherratt." A rare group. Price C. *Collection of Arnold and Barbara Berlin.*

Figure 133.7. Dandy and dandizette; with bocage. Attributed to Patriotic Group. H: ~8.2". Companion to the following example. Price C. *John Howard; www.antiquepottery.co.uk.*

Figure 133.8. Dandy and dandizette; with bocage. Attributed to Patriotic Group. H: 8.2". A companion to the previous example, with the couple in switched positions. Like it, it has a typical Patriotic Group bocage. Price C.

Figure 133.9. Dandy, dandizette, and dog; with bocage. Attributed to Patriotic Group. H: ~8.3". Like the previous example and, as expected on this model, the dandy clutches gloves. The previous example was made without the dog. Price C.

Figure 133.10. Dandy, dandizette, and dog; with bocage. Attributed to Patriotic Group. H: ~8.3". The addition of a small dog on the base is a charming touch. The dandy's basket is a restoration. Price C.

Figure 133.11. Dandy and dandizette. Possibly attributable to Patriotic Group. H: 8". Made without bocage. The dandy holds a reticule. The pattern on the base occurs on a group of musicians attributed to the Patriotic Group (Vol. 1, fig. 26.90). Price B.

Figure 133.12. Dandy and dandizette, reverse of previous example.

Figure 133.13. Dandy and dandizette. H: ~8.2". Made without bocage. Here the dandy's reticule has slipped from his grasp and is stuck to his coat. Price B. *Brighton and Hove Museums.*

Figure 133.14. Dandy and dandizette. H: 8.4". As in similar examples, there is no bocage and both figures have reticules. Price B. *Brighton and Hove Museums.*

Figure 133.15. Dandy and dandizette. H: ~8.2". Made without bocage. Like the previous example but painted quite differently. Price B.

Figure 133.16. Dandy and dandizette. H: ~8.2". Made without bocage. From the same molds as previous and following examples, but decorative differences impart great individuality. Price B. *Andrew Dando Antiques.*

Figure 133.17. Dandy and dandizette. H: ~8.2". Made without bocage. Price B. *www.madelena.com.*

Figure 133.18. Dandy and dandizette. H: 8.5"'. Made without bocage. Price B. *Peter Flemans.*

Figure 133.19. Dandy and dandizette. H: 8.3". Made without bocage. Groups of this form (with the lady to the left and wearing a longer dress) were probably companions to the immediately preceding examples that have the lady to the right. Price B. *Aurea Carter Antiques.*

Figure 133.20. Dandy and dandizette. H: 8". Made without bocage. Price B. *Brighton and Hove Museums.*

Figure 133.21. Dandy and dandizette. H: 8.7". Made without bocage. Again the dandizette stands on the left and wears an ankle length dress. Price B. *Collection of Arnold and Barbara Berlin.*

Figure 133.22. Dandy and dandizette. H: 8.5". Made without bocage. This couple staring adoringly into each other's eyes are known from only this example. Price C. *Saffron Walden Museum.*

Figure 133.23. Dandy and dandizette, a pair; with bocages. H: 8"(L), 7.5"(R). Dandy couples on individual bases are rare, and this is the only recorded example of this pair. Price D.

Figure 133.24. Dandy, detail of reverse of previous figure. The bocage fronds have hawthorn leaves arranged in threes. Flowers are on one bocage frond only.

Figure 133.25. Dandizette; with bocage. H: ~8". From the same figure molds as the previous dandizette but mounted on a square base. Price A.

Figure 133.26. Dandizette. H: ~7.8". From same figure molds as prior examples but on a different base and made without a bocage. Note the pink luster on her dress and the unusual dress pattern. Price A.

Figure 133.27. Dandizette; with bocage. Impressed "HALL". H: 7.3". Price B.

Figure 133.28. Dandizette; with bocage. Attributed to Hall. H: ~7.4". Like the previous dandizette and with a typical Hall bocage. Price A.

Figure 133.29. Dandy and dandizette, an assembled pair; with bocages. Impressed "HALL". H: ~7.5". Price C.

Figure 133.30. Dandy. Attributed to Dale. H: ~7". Made without bocage. The characteristic floral sprig on the base supports the attribution. Like the Hall dandy in figure 133.29, but Dale's dandy stands slightly further back on the base. Price B.

Figure 133.31. Dandy and dandizette, a pair, each with bocage. Probably made by Dale. H: ~7". The dandy is like the Dale dandy in figure 133.30, and the bocages are consistent with a Dale attribution. Price C.

Figure 133.32. Dandizette; with bocage. Probably made by Dale. H: ~7". The bocage (with restoration) is non-specific, but the base is as on the previous dandizette, and the figure is like the following Dale dandizette. Price B.

Figure 133.33. Dandizette. Attributed to Dale. H: 6.3".The bocage flowers and the base support the attribution. Companion to the following dandy. Price B. *Michael Goodacre.*

Figure 133.34. Dandy. Attributed to Dale. H: ~6.7". Bocage lost. Companion to the previous dandizette. Dale dandies are very like those made by Hall, but the Dale figures stand on tiptoes and slightly further back. Price A.

Figure 133.35. Dandy and dandizette. H: ~7". Made without bocages. These "skinny dandies" are very rare. Price D. *John Howard; www.antiquepottery.co.uk.*

Figure 133.36. Dandy and dandizette, reverse of previous pair. *John Howard; www.antiquepottery.co.uk.*

Figure 133.37. Dandy. H: 7". Made without bocage. From the same molds as the previous dandy but on a different base. Price B. *Saffron Walden Museum.*

Figure 133.38. Dandy; with bocage. H: 7". From the same molds as previous "skinny dandies," but made with a bocage. Price B. *Saffron Walden Museum.*

Figure 133.39. Dandy and dandizette; with bocage. Attributed to "Sherratt." H: 8". The bocage and floral sprigs applied to the base confirm the attribution. Pairs with the following example. Price C, pair.

Figure 133.40. Dandy and dandizette; with bocage. Attributed to "Sherratt." H: 7.9". Pairs with the previous example. Price C, pair.

Figure 133.41. Detail of the oak-leaf bocage on the previous dandies group. The flower clusters are each formed from a single mold.

Figure 133.42. Dandy and dandizette groups, reverse of the previous pair.

Figure 133.43. Pair of dandy and dandizette groups. Attributed to "Sherratt." H: ~6.5". From the same molds as used in the pairs in figs. 133.39–42 and 133.44 but made without bocages. The sprigs applied to the base confirm the attribution. Price C.

Figure 133.44. *THOMAS AND AN NAS, JOHN & MARY.* Pair of dandy and dandizette groups on table bases; with bocages. Attributed to "Sherratt." H: 10". As in previous Sherratt dandy pairs, the dandy of the right hand couple has a taller hat. The bases, titles, and floral sprigs are typical of "Sherratt." Price D.

Figure 133.45. Dandy and dandizette. H: ~8.2". Made without bocage. Like the right hand couple in the previous example but lacking features to support attribution. The sprigs on the base are non-specific. Price B.

Figure 133.46. Pair of dandy and dandizette groups; with bocages. Attributed to Patriotic Group. H: 6.7"(L), 6.5"(R). The sprig on the dandizette's basket, the dog's form, the bases, the painting style, and the fine dress patterns are consistent with the attribution. Price C.

Figure 133.47. Dandy and dandizette; with bocage. Attributed to Patriotic Group. H: ~8.4". Like the left hand couple in the previous pair but with a fuller bocage. Price B.

Figure 133.48. Dandy and dandizette; with bocage. Attributed to Patriotic Group. H: 7". Similar to the previous example but made without a dog. Price B. *Peter Flemans.*

Figure 133.49. Dandy and dandizette; with bocage. H: 7". Notable for the stunning enameling. Price C.

Figure 133.50. Dandy and dandizette; with bocage. H: 7". Similar to the previous example, but she holds a reticule rather than an umbrella. Price B. *John Howard; www.antiquepottery.co.uk.*

Figure 133.51. Dandy and dandizette; with bocage. H: 7". Like the previous two examples but enameled differently. Her reticule is attached to her dress, rather than to her hand. Price B. *W. W. Warner Antiques.*

Figure 133.52. Dandy and dandizette. H: 6.8". Made without bocage. Price B. *John Howard; www.antiquepottery.co.uk.*

Figure 133.53. Dandy and dandizette, reverse of previous example. *John Howard; www. antiquepottery.co.uk.*

Figure 133.54. Dandy and dandizette. H: 6.7". Made without bocage. Like the previous group but the base differs. In groups in this style, the lady wears a large bonnet when she stands on the left and a flatter hat when standing on the right. Price B. *Nick Burton.*

Figure 133.55. Dandy and dandizette; with bocage. H: ~7". Price B. *Andrew Dando Antiques.*

Figure 133.56. Dandy and dandizette; with bocage. H: ~6.5". Price B.

Figure 133.57. Dandy and dandizette; with bocage. H: 6.3". Note the unusual dog. A companion to the following couple. Price B. *Michael Goodacre.*

Figure 133.58. Dandy and dandizette; with bocage. H: 6.9". A companion to the previous couple, having the same base, unusual dog, and baskets, but the bocage fronds differ. Price B. *John Howard; www.antiquepottery.co.uk.*

Figure 133.59. Dandy and dandizette; with bocage. H: ~8". The bocage (five-leaflet fern fronds) is above the dandies' heads. In most groups of this size, the bocage is to either side. Price B. *Elinor Penna.*

Figure 133.60. Dandy and dandizette; with bocage. H: ~8". This couple is from slightly different molds than most, and the base is different. The bocage is restored. Price A.

Figure 133.61. Dandy and dandizette; with bocage. H: 8.3". Attributed to Leather Leaf Group. The base and the bocage leaves and acorns are characteristic of the Group. Companion to the following couple. Price B. *Whitehall Antiques, Chapel Hill, North Carolina.*

Figure 133.62. Dandy and dandizette; with bocage. H: ~8.5". Attributed to Leather Leaf Group. The base and the bocage leaves and flowers are characteristic of the Group. Companion to the previous couple. Price B.

Figure 133.63. Dandy and dandizette; with bocage. H: 8.3". Attributed to Leather Leaf Group. Like the previous example but painted differently and with a characteristic starfish-like flower on the base. Price B.

Figure 133.64. Dandy and dandizette. H: 6". Made without bocage. Atypical in that the lady wears a small hat but stands to the left. Note their alarmed expressions. Price A. *Peter Flemans.*

Figure 133.65. Dandy and dandizette, reverse of previous pair. *Peter Flemans.*

Figure 136.66. Dandy and dandizette. H: 6.7". Made without bocage. Note that both the dandy and dandizette wear the high starched collars normally worn by only the gentleman. Price A. *www.madelena.com.*

Figure 133.67. Dandy and dandizette; with bocage. H: 4.8". An unusual dumpy little couple. Price B.

Figure 133.68. Dandy and dandizette; with bocage. H: 5". These figures are like the bride and groom within New Marriage Act arbor groups. Price B.

Figure 133.69. Dandy and dandizette. H: 3.2". Like the previous example in that these figures are also the bride and groom in New Marriage Act arbors. With losses. Price A. *Image courtesy of The Potteries Museum & Art Gallery, Stoke-on-Trent, UK.*

Figure 133.70. Dandy and dandizette; with bocage. Attributed to Leaf Mat Group. H: ~5". Price A.

Figure 133.71. Dandy and dandizette; with bocage. Probably made by Dale. H: 4.9". The bocage leaves and flowers and the scrolling on the base suggest the attribution. The figures lack necks. Price A.

Figure 133.72. Dandy and dandizette; with bocage. Probably made by Dale. H: 4.9". The base, bocage (tips restored), and partial flower are as in the previous example, but here the figures have distinct necks. Price A.

Figure 133.73. Dandy and dandizette; with bocage. Attributed to Blue Group. H: 4.9". The five-petalled flowers are characteristic of the Group. Price A. *The William Herbert and Nancy Hunt Collection.*

Figure 133.74. *DANDIES* (impressed on base). Dandy and dandizette; with bocage. H: ~4.4". Attributed to Patriotic Group. The bocage flowers are specific to the Group. Price A. *Michael Goodacre.*

Figure 133.75. *DANDIES* (impressed on base). Dandy and dandizette; with bocage. Attributed to Patriotic Group. H: ~4.4". The same titled base as the previous couple. These bocage fronds and flowers occur on other Patriotic Group examples. Price A.

Figure 133.76. Dandy and dandizette; with bocage. Attributed to "Sherratt." H: ~4". The bocage flowers (usually found elsewhere on "Sherratt" figures) and her cockade (a frequent "Sherratt" feature) support the attribution. Price A.

Figure 133.77. Dandy and dandizette. Attributed to "Sherratt." H: ~4". Made without bocage. Like the previous example and painted similarly. Price A.

Figure 133.78. Dandy and dandizette. H: 4". Made without bocage. Price A.

Figure 133.79. Dandy and dandizette. H: ~3.7". Made without bocage. On a different base from previous small couples. Price A.

Figure 133.80. Dandy and dandizette. H: ~3.8". Made without bocage. Price A. *Andrew Dando Antiques.*

Figure 133.81. Dandy and dandizette. H: ~3.7". Made without bocage. From the same molds as the previous couple. Price A. *www.madelena.com.*

134. The Assassination of Marat

In 1765, Jean-Paul Marat (1743–1793), a Frenchman of Swiss birth, set up as a physician in London, despite lack of formal qualifications. In 1770, he became a veterinarian in Newcastle upon Tyne and while there wrote his first political work. But Marat incurred heavy debt and was sentenced to five years of hard labor for stealing gold coins and medallions from Oxford's Ashmolean Museum. The 1780s found Marat in Paris, where he emerged as an architect and leader of the bloody Reign of Terror that swept France. On July 13, 1793, Charlotte Corday, blaming Marat for the mass misery and the steady stream of guillotine victims, visited his home armed with a six-inch kitchen knife and stabbed him to death. Just four days later, on July 17, 1793, Charlotte Corday, aged 24, went to the guillotine for her crime. During her trial, she stated "I have slain one man to save a hundred thousand."[1]

Charlotte Corday must have become a heroine among Britain's better classes when she silenced one of the French Revolution's most prominent mouthpieces. Depictions of Marat's murder quickly appeared in print shop windows in 1793, but the print that is the design source for the figure appears to be *The Death of Marat, Late Member of the National Convention, at Paris, on the 13th of July 1793*, published by Robert Sayer in November 1793.

Figure 134.1. *The Death of Marat, Late Member of the National Convention, at Paris, on the 13th of July 1793.* Published by Robert Sayer, November 1793. © *Trustees of the British Museum.*

Figure 134.2. *The Afsafsination of MARAT, by CHARLOTTE. CORDE' of Ca'en, in Normandy. 1793.* Impressed "LAKIN & POOLE". H: 13.6". Note the gilding on her clothing and jewelry. Price D. *Bonhams.*

135. The Death of Munrow

The Death of Munrow commemorates the death of Lt. Hugh Munro, and the misspelling of the Munro name occurs on all titled examples. Lt. Munro was a young army officer who was savaged by a tiger while hunting deer in India in 1792. Tipu, the sultan of Mysore, hated the British, and he owned a life-sized automaton depicting a tiger savaging a British army officer. While it is convenient to think that Tipu had the automaton made to commemorate the death of his young enemy, in truth he may have owned the automaton at the time that Munro met his fate. In 1799, Tipu fell in battle, and British forces captured the automaton. The automaton—now known as *Tippoo's Tiger*, "Tippoo" being the contemporary spelling of the sultan's name—was shipped back to London, where it was displayed at India House from 1808. Because there was considerable public interest in Britain's conquest of Mysore, Tippoo's Tiger soon became a popular tourist attraction, and it probably inspired The Death of Munrow. An engraving of a tiger by Thomas Bewick commissioned for a menagerie poster probably assisted in modeling the beast.[1]

The Death of Munrow groups are impressive and are avidly sought by collectors. They are infrequent and command consistently high prices. Currently, the price record for figures of this period is held by a *The Death of Munrow* that sold for $153,600 at Sotheby's, New York, on April 7, 2004. Some examples have superior enamels and glazes and are painted with greater attention to detail, and this should impact price. Most commonly, the group occurs on titled table bases, but variations in tail position, base type, and decoration occur. A black tiger on a table base is shown. In 1827, Shore's Royal Menagerie advertised its black tiger as "the only one ever seen in the Kingdom,"[2] and the beast probably inspired that figure group.

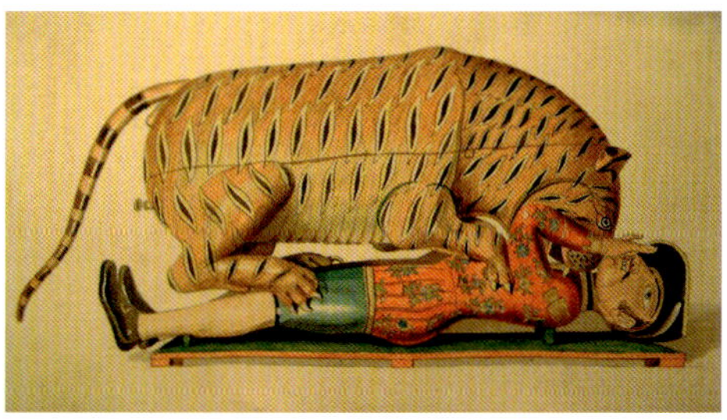

Figure 135.1. Tippoo's Tiger. Engraved by W. Cooke, circa 1800.

Figure 135.2. *THE DEATH OF MUNROW*. H: 11.5", L: 14". Attributed to "Sherratt." The green pattern painted atop the table base also occurs on an example of *THE RORING LION*. Possibly such groups were intended as companion pieces. Price G. *Collection of Arnold and Barbara Berlin.*

Figure 135.3. *THE DEATH OF MUNROW.* L: ~14". Attributed to "Sherratt." Like the previous example but with simpler painting. This is the most common base on this group. Price G.

Figure 135.4. *The Death of Munrow.* Attributed to "Sherratt." H: 10.9", L: 14". This very pretty base is uncommon on this group. A "Sherratt" *Roaring Lion* with a similar base has been recorded, and the two groups may have been intended as companions. Price G.

Figure 135.5. *THE DEATH OF MUNROW*. L ~14.6". Attributed to "Sherratt." The tiger's tail is sometimes tucked, as correctly shown in this example. Price G. *Moore Collection.*

Figure 135.6. *THE DEATH OF MUNROW*. L ~14.6". Attributed to "Sherratt." The brown base differs from the previous brown base in that it has clawed feet. The tiger's tail is restored. Price G.

Figure 135.7. *The Death of Munrow.* Probably made by "Sherratt." H: 9.3", L: 14". This group lacks specific "Sherratt" features but may have been made by "Sherratt." Price G. *Brighton and Hove Museums.*

Figure 135.8. *The Death of Munrow.* Attributed to "Sherratt." L: ~14". The base is of the same form as the brown clawed base in figure 135.6. Price G.

Figure 135.9. *THE DEATH OF MUNROW.* L: ~14". Attributed to "Sherratt." In 1827, Shore's Royal Menagerie advertised its black tiger (probably a leopard), and that beast possibly inspired this black tiger. Price G. *Photograph Courtesy of Sotheby's, Inc. © 2014.*

136. Menagerie Deaths

On February 18,1834, as Wombwell's travelling menagerie rested overnight, a tigress and a lion named Wallace escaped from their cages. The two felines attacked and killed four people, including a mother with a child in her arms. The event is documented in the *Northampton Herald* of February 22, 1834, and in a broadside sourced from the *Northampton Herald*, now in the National Library of Scotland. The following day, the animals were fined £10 for "Accidental Death." George Wombwell, the menagerie proprietor, quickly stepped forward to cover all expenses, including funeral costs, and he probably did all he could to ensure that word of this escapade did not spread. The tragedy took place at Worksworth, just a short distance from the Potteries, and the chilling news must have inspired potters to capture the events in clay.[1]

Today, a handful of very rare figures depict the menagerie deaths. Figure 136.1, aptly titled *MENAGERIE*, portrays the fate of the "woman with a child in her arms" described in the *Northampton Herald*. Although the newspaper does not state the race of the victims, one gentleman must have been of African descent because three figure groups attest to the mauling of a black male (figs. 136.3, 136.5–6).

Figure 136.1. *MENAGERIE*. Tigress with a baby dangling from its jaws and mauling a lady. Attributed to "Sherratt." H: 6.6". From molds used in several other "Sherratt" groups. The title pertains to the fact that the tigress had escaped from Wombwell's menagerie. Price F.

Figure 136.2. Lion mauling a lady; with bocage. Attributed to "Sherratt." L: ~7.5". Portrays Wallace, the famous menagerie lion. Pairs with the following example. Price E. *Bonhams*.

Figure 136.3. Tiger mauling a black man; with bocage. Attributed to "Sherratt." L: ~7.8". Pairs with the previous group. Price E. *Bonhams*.

Figure 136.4. Lion mauling a child. Attributed to "Sherratt." H: 5.5", L: 8.2". This base is specific to "Sherratt." Price E. *The William Herbert and Nancy Hunt Collection.*

Figure 136.5. *THE DEATH OF A NEGRO*. Attributed to "Sherratt." L: 12.6". The figure of a black man is lacking. This spotted feline is probably intended to be a tiger. Like the tiger used in *THE DEATH OF MUNROW* groups, but the base is not as deep. Price F. *Waddington's, Toronto.*

Figure 136.6. Tiger mauling a black man. H: 8.5", L: 17". Price F. *Image courtesy of The Potteries Museum & Art Gallery, Stoke-on-Trent, UK.*

137. The Red Barn Murder

On May 18, 1827, Maria Marten met William Corder at the barn on his family farm in Polstead, Suffolk. The barn was known as the "red barn" because it appeared red in certain light. The couple was supposed to go to Ipswich to marry, but William murdered Maria and buried her body beneath the barn floor. The location of the body was revealed to Maria's stepmother in a psychic dream, and William—happily married and living elsewhere—was arrested and tried for murder. In August 1828, he was hanged at a public spectacle witnessed by thousands. The Red Barn Murder is a tale replete with unanswered questions and salacious details. As the crime of its era, it received extensive news coverage and it inspired melodramas and narratives. In the twentieth century, it provided material for plays, investigative literature, and a movie.[1]

Contemporary engravings of Maria Marten and William Corder assisted in modeling the earthenware figures. All Red Barn figures and groups are rare. Their scarcity supports the belief that pre-Victorian earthenware figures were made for respectable, upwardly aspiring households, where the Red Barn Murder was a distasteful subject.

Figure 137.1. *The Red Barn at Polstead*. From *The Mysterious Murder of Maria Marten*, 1828. Earthenware Red Barns resemble this barn.

Figure 137.2. *A VIEW OF THE RED BARN AT POULSTON*. H: 6.4", L: 7.1". Most Red Barns link to "Sherratt," but this example was made by another pot bank from quite different molds. Price E.

Figure 137.3. Detail of figures on the previous Red Barn. Both figures are original.

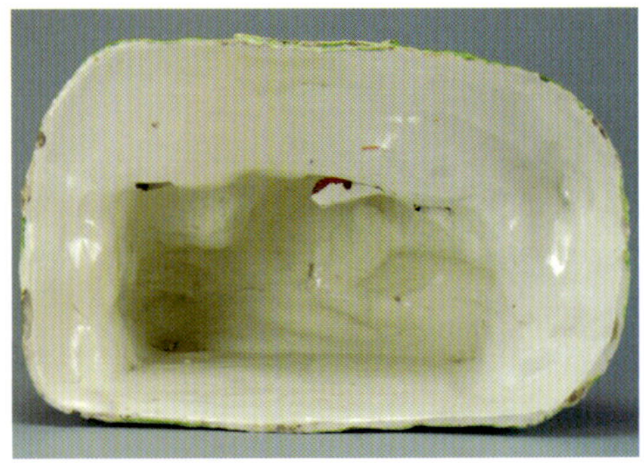

Figure 137.4. The Red Barn, previous example, from beneath.

Figure 137.5. The Red Barn, reverse of previous example.

Figure 137.6. *A VIEW OF THE RED BARN AT POLSTEAD*. H: 6", L: 7.5". Like the previous example. Three similar Red Barns are recorded, each with a different spelling of Polstead.[2] This bocage with these flowers is on figures 31.31 and 103.2 in Volume 2. Price E. *The William Herbert and Nancy Hunt Collection.*

Figure 137.7. *THE RED BARN*. Attributed to "Sherratt." H: 8.8". Most "Sherratt" Red Barns have this brown footed base. Animals and figures are frequently lost or restored, but here they are all original. Price D. *Bonhams.*

Figure 137.8. *THE RED BARN*. Attributed to "Sherratt." H: ~9". The base and the floral sprigs on it support attribution. Price D. *John Howard; www.antiquepottery.co.uk.*

Figure 137.9. The figure of Maria Marten on the previous Red Barn. This figure is original, but Red Barn figures are frequently lost and a replica is put in its place.

Figure 137.10. *THE RED BARN*. Attributed to "Sherratt." H: ~8.5". Like previous examples but with a "Sherratt" double anthemion bocage. The figures are restored. Price B.

Figure 137.11. *THE RED BARN*. Attributed to "Sherratt." H: ~9". The traditional "Sherratt" Red Barn but with yet another bocage form. The cow and the bocage fronds touching the roof are original; the rest of the bocage and the other figures are restored. Price B.

Figure 137.12. *THE RED BARN*. Attributed to "Sherratt." H: 8", L: 12". On a different "Sherratt" base from previous examples and with a typical "Sherratt" bocage with oak leaves and mayflowers. Price C. *John Howard; www.antiquepottery.co.uk.*

Figure 137.13. *THE RED BARN NEAR POLSTEAD BURY ST EDMUNDS*. Attributed to Patriotic Group. H: 8.3". The pinecone bocage is exclusive to the Patriotic Group. This Red Barn model was made without figures of Corder and Marten. Price D. © *Christie's Images Limited 2014.*

Figure 137.14. *THE RED BARN*. Attributed to "Sherratt." H: 4.5", L: 4.9". Known only from this example. The base and the titling support the attribution. Price E.

Figure 137.15. Detail of figures on the previous Red Barn. These figures are not known in any other context.

Figure 137.16. *THE RED BARN*, reverse of previous example.

Figure 137.17. *W. CORDER & M. MARTEN, THE RED BARN, W CORDER BEFORE THE JUDGE.* Attributed to "Sherratt." H: 8", 8.8", 7.7". A spectacular set that appears to have been together since manufacture. Original condition. Price F. *Bonhams.*

Figure 137.18. Engraving of William Corder standing before the judge. From *The Red Barn* by William Maginn, 1828.

Figure 137.19. *W CORDER BEFORE THE JUDGE.* Attributed to "Sherratt." H: 7.7". The only recorded example. Part of a set (fig. 137.17).

Figure 137.20. *Corder.* Probably made by "Sherratt." H: 6.4". From the same molds as the previous figure but with no characteristics to support attribution. Price B.

Figure 137.21. *Maria Marten*. From *The Mysterious Murder of Maria Marten*, 1828.

Figure 137.22. *W. CORDER & M. MARTEN*. Attributed to "Sherratt." H: 7.9". This couple also occurs on a square base with canted corners, with the title impressed directly into the base and the figures' arms positioned differently. Price D. *Brighton and Hove Museums*.

Figure 137.23. *W CORDER BEFORE THE JUDGE. W CORDER & M MARTEN*. Attributed to "Sherratt." H: 9.5". Price E. *The William Herbert and Nancy Hunt Collection*.

In addition to the examples shown here, the author has noted a "Sherratt" figure group showing Maria Marten and William Corder standing on either side of a bulbous spill vase. The vase has a clock face; the base is banded with two painted lines, and a plaque on the base reads *"W CORDER & M MARTEN."*

Notes

111. Performing Animals
1. Myrna Schkolne. *People, Passions, Pastimes, and Pleasures: Staffordshire Figures 1810–1835.* (Winston-Salem, NC: Hot Lane Press, 2006), pp. 116–125.
2. Patricia Halfpenny and Stella Beddoe. *Circus and Sport*. (Louisville, KY: J.B. Speed Art Museum, 1990), 19.

112. Menageries
1. Thomas Frost. *The Old Showmen, and the Old London Fairs.* (London: Tinsely, 1874), p. 277.
2. Rodney Hampson. *Pottery References in the Staffordshire Advertiser, 1795–1865.* (Hanley: Northern Ceramic Society, 2000), p. 92.
3. Edward H Bostock. *Menageries, Circuses, and Theatres.* (London: Chapman & Hall, 1928), p. 5.
4. Examples are in the Newcastle-under-Lyme Museum and the Fitzwilliam Museum, and in private collections.

115. Camels
1. Halfpenny and Beddoe. *Circus and Sport*, p. 12.
2. James Rennie. *The Menageries: Quadrupeds, Described and Drawn from Living Species*. (London, Knight, 1829–1840), pp. 217–218.
3. Ibid, pp. 309–310.

122. Elephants
1. Leslie Grigsby. *English Pottery 1650–1800: The Henry K. Weldon Collection.* (London: Sotheby's Publications, 1990), p. 384.
2. Christie's South Kensington, October 26, 2000, lot 41.

125. Horses
1. Bonhams London, September 9, 2009, lot 23.

131. Sheep
1. Thomas Bewick. *A General History of Quadrupeds.* (England: Smith, 1980), p. 53.
2. *Register of Arts, and Journal of Patent Invention,* ed. by L. Herbert. "Annual Consumption of London." (London: Steill, 1828), p. 303.

134. The Assassination of Marat
1. L. H. Young. *The Historical Cabinet: Containing Authentic Accounts of Many Remarkable and Interesting Events.* (New Haven: Young, 1834), p. 13

135. The Death of Munrow
1. Schkolne. *People, Passions, Pastimes, and Pleasures*, p. 40.
2. *Collection of Cuttings from Newspapers, Advertisements, Playbills, etc, Formed by Fillinham. pp. 6-8. Trained Animals, Menageries, etc.* (Held in the British Library.)

136. Menagerie Deaths
1. Schkolne. *People, Passions, Pastimes, and Pleasures*, pp. 112–113.

137. The Red Barn Murders
1. Schkolne. *People, Passions, Pastimes, and Pleasures*, pp. 46–53.
2. A Red Barn of this form is in the Willett Collection, *Brighton and Hove Museums.*

Bibliography

Bewick, Thomas. *A General History of Quadrupeds.* England: Smith, 1980.

Bradshaw, Peter. *18th Century English Porcelain Figures.* Woodbridge, Suffolk: Antique Collectors' Club, 1981.

------. *Derby Porcelain Figures 1750–1848.* London: Faber & Faber, 1990.

Bostock, Edward H. *Menageries, Circuses, and Theatres.* London: Chapman & Hall, 1928.

Collection of Cuttings from Newspapers, Advertisements, Playbills, etc., Formed by Fillinham. 6-8. Trained Animals, Menageries, etc. Held in the British Library.

Cox, Alwyn and Angela Cox. *Rockingham 1745–1842.* Woodbridge, Suffolk: Antique Collectors' Club, 2001.

Dudson, Audrey M. and Alison Morgan. *Dudson Staffordshire Figures.* Stoke-on-Trent: Dudson Publications, 2006.

Earle, Cyril. *The Earle Collection of Early Staffordshire Pottery.* London: Brown, 1915.

Edwards Diana. *Neale Pottery and Porcelain, its Predecessors and Successors 1763–1829.* London: Barrie & Jenkins 1987.

Edwards, Diana and Rodney Hampson. *English Dry-Bodied Stoneware: Wedgwood and Contemporary Manufacturers 1774–1830.* Woodbridge, Suffolk: Antique Collectors' Club, 1998.

Falkner, Frank. *The Wood Family of Burslem.* London: Chapman & Hall, 1912.

Godden, Geoffrey A. *Encyclopaedia of British Pottery and Porcelain Marks.* London: Barrie & Jenkins, 1991.

Goodacre, J.M. *A Catalogue of the Goodacre Collection of Early Staffordshire Pottery Figures.* N.p.: Goodacre, 2007.

Frost, Thomas. *The Old Showmen, and the Old London Fairs.* London: Tinsely, 1874.

Grigsby, Leslie. *English Pottery 1650 1800: The Henry K. Weldon Collection.* London: Sotheby's Publications, 1990.

Haggar, Reginald. *Staffordshire Chimney Ornaments.* London: Phoenix House, 1955.

Halfpenny, Pat. *English Earthenware Figures 1780–1840.* Woodbridge, Suffolk: Antique Collectors' Club, 1991.

Halfpenny, Patricia and Stella Beddoe. *Circus and Sport.* Louisville, KY: J.B. Speed Art Museum, 1990.

Hall, John, *Staffordshire Portrait Figures.* New York: World Pub., 1972.

Hamilton-Foyn, Wynne. "Who Modelled and Made Ralph Wood Figures?" Unpublished research, 2009. Held at the Victoria and Albert Museum, British Museum, Potteries Museum, Fitzwilliam Museum, Ashmolean Museum, and Wedgwood Museum.

Hampson, Rodney. *Pottery References in the Staffordshire Advertiser, 1795–1865.* Hanley: Northern Ceramic Society, 2000.

Hayden, Arthur. *Chats on English Earthenware.* London: Unwin, 1909.

Henrywood, R. K. *Staffordshire Potters 1781–1900.* Woodbridge: Antique Collectors' Club, 2002.

Hodkinson, H. M. and Judith Hodkinson. *Sherratt? A Natural Family of Staffordshire Figures.* London: Chisquare, 1991.

Horne, Jonathan. *A Collection of Early English Pottery, parts I to X 1981–1990.* London: Jonathan Horne, 1981–1990.

------. *A Collection of Early English Pottery, parts XI to XX 1991–2000.* London: Jonathan Horne, 1991–2000.

Hughes, J. F. *Recollections of Old Liverpool by a Nonagerian.* Liverpool, 1836.

Jewitt, Llewellynn. *The Wedgwoods: being a life of Josiah Wedgwood; with notices of his works and their productions, memoirs of the Wedgewood and other families, and a history of the early potteries of Staffordshire.* London, Virtue., 1865.

Jewitt, Llewellynn. *The Ceramic Art of Great Britain.* N.p: Virtue, 1878.

Kiddell, A. J. B. "William Absolon of Yarmouth," *English Ceramic Circle Transactions*, 5:1 (1960), 53–64.

John, W. D., and Warren Baker. *Old English Lustre Ware.* New York: Walker, 1966.

Lewis, Griselda. *A Collector's History of English Pottery.* Woodbridge, Suffolk: Antique Collectors' Club, 1985.

Lewis, John, and Griselda Lewis. *Pratt Ware: English and Scottish Relief Decorated and Underglaze Coloured Earthenware.* Woodbridge, Suffolk: Antique Collectors' Club, 2006.

Locket, T. A. and P. A. Halfpenny, eds. *Creamware and Pearlware Re-Examined.* Stoke-on-Trent, City Museum and Art Gallery, 1989.

Manheim, Emily. *Selections from the Hope McCormick Collection of Staffordshire Pottery.* Chicago, 1980.

McVeigh, Patrick. *Scottish East Coast Potteries.* Edinburgh: Donald, 1979.

Oliver, Anthony. *Staffordshire Pottery: the Tribal Art of England.* London: Heinemann, 1981.

Poole, Julia. *Plagiarism Personified.* Cambridge: Fitzwilliam Museum, 1986.

Price, R. K. *Astbury, Whieldon, and Ralph Wood Figures, and Toby Jugs.* London: John Lane, 1992.

Pugh, P. D. *Gordon, Staffordshire Portrait Figures of the Victorian Age.* Woodbridge, Suffolk: Antique Collectors' Club, 1987.

Rackham, Bernard. *Catalogue of the Glaisher Collection of Pottery & Porcelain in the Fitzwilliam Museum, Cambridge.* Woodbridge, Suffolk: Antique Collectors' Club, 1987.

Read, Herbert. *Staffordshire Pottery Figures.* London: Duckworth, 1929.

Register of Arts, and Journal of Patent Invention, ed. by L. Herbert. "Annual Consumption of London." London: Steill, 1828.

Rennie, James. *The Menageries: Quadrupeds, Described and Drawn from Living Species, vol. 1.* London, Knight, 1829–1840.

Roden, Peter. *Copyhold Potworks and Housing in the Staffordshire Potteries, 1700–1832.* Cumbria: Wood Broughton Publications, 2008.

Schkolne, Myrna. "A Pearlware Puzzle: Walton Figures and Their Look-Alikes," *American Ceramic Circle Journal*, XVI (2011), 56–77.

--------. *People, Passions, Pastimes, and Pleasures: Staffordshire Figures 1810–1835.* Winston-Salem, NC: Hot Lane Press, 2006.

Stanley, Louis T. *Collecting Staffordshire Pottery.* New York: Doubleday, 1963.

Staffordshire Education Dept. *A Directory of the Staffordshire Potteries.* Stafford: Staffordshire County Council, 1982.

Ward, John. The Borough of Stoke-upon-Trent. London: Lewis, 1843.

Walton, Peter. *Creamware and Other English Pottery at Temple Newsam House, Leeds.* Bradford, UK, Manningham, 1976.

Williams, Peter, and Pat Halfpenny. *A Passion for Pottery.* New York: Sotheby's, 2000.

Young, L. H. *The Historical Cabinet: Containing Authentic Accounts of Many Remarkable and Interesting Events.* New Haven: Young, 1834.

Index

Italics denote titled figures
The number in **bold font** preceding page numbers indicates the relevant Volume number

Abraham, *See* Offering of Isaac
Absolon, William, **1**: 28; **2**: 238
Actaeon, **1**: 16
Adonis, **1**: 21
Aesculapius, **1**: 31
African Sal, **2**: 76
Agrippina, **2**: 47, 48
Ainsworth, William Harrison, **2**: 78, 79
Air, figures emblematic of, **1**: 17.
Ale Bench, **3**: 11
Alexander, Czar, **1**: 18, 22
Andrew, Saint, **1**: 27, **2**: 218, 219
Anteros, **1**: 21; **3**: 16
Anthony, Mark, **2**: 24, 25
Apollo, **1**: 14, 16, 21, 26, 27, 28
archer, **1**: 17; **2**: 136, 137
Ariadne, **1**: 14, 21, 273
Arinette, **2**: 60
Assassination of Marat, **1**: 14; **3**: 259
Astley, Philip, **2**: 5
Austin, William, **1**: 28
Autumn, figures emblematic of, **1**: 16, 24, 28. *See also* seasons
Bacchus, **1**: 16
Bacon, John, **3**: 148
Bag Piper, **1**: 26, 163
bagpiper. *See* musician
Bakewell, Robert, **3**: 46
Ballad Singer, **1**: 253
Barbara, Saint, **2**: 220
Barber & Mate, **1**: 236
barber, **1**: 238, 239
Barker, Sutton, & Till, **1**: 28
barmaid, **1**: 240, 241
Barrymore, Lady, **2**: 125
bear, **3**: 179. *See also* bear baiting, dancing bear
bear baiting; **2**: 126–128
Berry, Edward, **1**: 28
Bertrand, Mary, **2**: 47
Bewick, Thomas, **3**: 185, 257
Big Blossom Group, **1**: 41
  figures by, **1**: 41, 112, 123; **2**: 170, 171; **3**: 71, 95, 204
bird, **3**: 16–29
Bird Catchers, **1**: 154; **3**: 31
bird, people with, **3**: 30–36
birds nest, people holding, **1**: 11, 274
blacksmith, **1**: 243
Blue Group, **1**: 29
  figures by, **1**: 29, 49, 72, 115, 180, 198, 213, 214, 271, 272; **2**: 14, 228, 232, 237; **3**: 98, 194–196, 254
bocage in socket, **1**: 9; **2**: 151, 152, 213; **3**: 53, 124
bocage leaves, shapes of, **1**: 6
Boccaccio, Giovanni, **2**: 43
Bonaparte, Napoleon, **2**: 108, 128
Bott & Co., **1**: 28
box, **3**: 20, 128, 173
Boxing Baroness, **2**: 125
Box Title Group, **1**: 30
  figures by, **1**: 30, 49, 62, 91, 116, 123, 127, 197, 198, 228, 229; **2**: 54, 79, 178, 214, 225, 238, 239, 247, 248; **3**: 96, 97, 116, 205
boxer, **2**:120–125
Boy and Dog. *See* shepherd
Brameld, John and William, **1**: 28; **2**: 52; **3**: 85
Britannia, **1**: 22; **2**: 81, 82, 121
Broom Lady, **2**: 62–64
Brown Base Group, **1**: 14, 31
  figures by, **1**: 31
Buddha, **2**: 263
bull. *See* cow, bull baiting
bull baiting, **1**: 26, 28; **2**: 129–135
Bunbury, Henry, **2**: 30
Burdett, Francis, **1**: 253
Burns, Robert, **2**: 38
butcher, **1**: 246
Butler, Samuel, **2**: 50
By a Broom, **2**: 64
By a Vach, **1**: 251
Caldwell, James. *See* Wood & Caldwell
camel, **1**: 24; **3**: 37, 38
canary. *See* bird
Cartledge, John, **1**: 28
cat, **3**: 39–43, 175
cat, people with, **3**: 44, 45
Cephalus & Procris, **1**: 14
Ceres, **1**: 16, 22, 28, 30
Charity, **1**: 18, 21, 24, 274; **2**: 183–194
Charlotte at the tomb of Werther, **1**: 24; **2**: 41, 42
Chaucer, Geoffrey **1**: 27, 274; **2**: 100, 101
Cheere, John, **2**: 99
Chetham and Woolley, **2**: 190
chimney sweep, **1**: 26, 27, 247, 248
Christ. *See* Jesus
Christ's Agony, **2**: 163, 164
Chunee, **3**: 136
Cimon. *See* Roman Charity, Cymon
Clarence, Duke of, **1**: 28; **2**: 93
Cleopatra, **1**: 16; **2**: 24, 25
Cleoptra, **1**: 21; **2**: 25
Clowes, William, **1**: 28
Clown, **1**: 26, 247; **2**: 22, 23
cobbler, **1**: 238
cockerel, **3**: 24–26
Cock Fighters, **3**: 35
Coffey, Charles, **2**: 52
Columbine, **2**: 57, 59
Combe, William, **2**: 31, 34
comedia dell'arte, **2**: 57
Contest, **1**: 27
Copeland & Garrett, **3**: 40
Corday, Charlotte, **3**: 256
Corder, William, **3**: 261–267
Cossack, **2**: 15
Cottage Boy, Cottage Girl, **1**: 94
coursing, **2**: 152, 153
cow with iron tail. *See* water pump
cow, **1**: 9, 32, 42; **3**: 46–66
cow, people with. *See* milkmaid
Cribb, Thomas, **2**: 122–124
Cromwell, Oliver, **1**: 26; **2**: 94
crucifixion, **2**: 166, 167
Cumberland, Duke of, **2**: 89
Cupid and Psyche, **1**: 14
Cup Lady, **3**: 51
Cup Toyda, **3**: 51
Cyfflé, Paul Louis, **2**: 22, 43
Cymon, **1**: 21, 27; **2**: 43, 45
Czar Alexander. *See* Alexander
Daisy Group, **1**: 41
  figures by, **1**: 41, 61, 173, 186, 18; **3**: 53, 70, 161, 203
Dale, John, **1**: 7–9, 31
  figures by, **1**: 7, 9, 74, 80, 91, 99, 105, 106, 114, 117, 118, 127, 166, 168, 185, 186, 193, 194, 218, 219, 268; **2**: 140, 141, 150, 151, 164, 172, 181, 213; **3**: 30, 37, 53, 54, 63, 74, 100, 101, 104, 124, 157, 188, 203, 237, 245, 246, 254
Dale, William, **1**: 7
dame school, **1**: 97
dancing bear, **3**: 5–8
dancing dogs, **3**: 5, 10
dandies, **3**: 240–255
David, King. *See* King David
death of Marat. See *Assassination of Marat*
Death of Munrow, **3**: 257–258
deer, **1**: 39, 40, 43; **3**: 67–107
deer stalker, **2**: 152
Defoe, Daniel, **2**: 79
Demosthenes, **1**: 22
Departure, **2**: 112
Diana, **1**: 24, 26, 28
Dixon, Austin, & Co. **1**: 28
Dixon, Robert, **1**: 28
Doctor Syntax, **2**: 31–37
dog, **1**: 30, 32; **2**: 150; **3**: 108–128. *See also* dancing dogs
Dog of Alcibiades, **3**: 108, 109
dog, people with, **3**: 129–135. *See also* shepherd
dolphin, **3**: 181
donkey, **3**: 146
Douglas, **2**: 73–75
dovecote, **3**: 16
Dr. Franklin. *See* Franklin, Benjamin
Dray Men, **1**: 241, 242
dromedary, **3**: 37
Dudson Family, **1**: 10
  figures by, **1**: 10, 61, 62, 79, 81, 133, 134, 154, 160, 161, 164, 177, 205, 222, 232; **2**: 17, 21, 147, 148, 170, 205, 209, 243; **3**: 17, 30, 31, 35, 36, 52, 74, 88, 94, 95, 99, 114, 120, 223, 224
Dudson, Richard, **1**: 10
Duncan, Admiral, **1**: 28
Dusty Bob, **1**: 24; **2**: 76
Dutch boy, **1**: 27, 252
Dutch girl, **1**: 27, 252
eagle, **1**: 21; **3**: 22–23
Edge & Grocott, **1**: 11, 38
  figures by, **1**: 11, 181, 192
Edge, Daniel, **1**: 11, 38
Edge, Timothy, **1**: 11
Egan, Pierce, **2**: 73, 76
elephant, **3**: 136–138
Elijah, **1**: 13, 26, 27; **2**: 168–181
Emanuel, Saint, **2**: 218
equestrian. *See* horse with rider
Eros, **1**: 21; **3**: 16
Eve, **2**: 182
Faith, **1**: 21, 24; **2**: 183–194
falconer, **1**: 27; **2**: 153–155
Falstaff, **1**: 22, 273; **2**: 28–30
Fanelli, Francesco, **2**: 83
Farewell, **2**: 111
farm worker, **1**: 32, 220–234
Father, If Thou Be Willing..., **2**: 164
Fayd'herbe, Lucas, **2**: 241
Fell, Thomas, **1**: 28; **3**: 174
fisherwoman, **1**: 243, 244
Flemish Music. **1**: 25, 27, 156, 157, 160
Flight to Egypt, **2**: 195–201
Flora, **1**: 21
Foote, Maria, **2**: 60
Fortitude, **1**: 21, 22
Fortune, **1**: 27, 274
Foster, John, **1**: 21, 28
fowl. *See* bird
fox, **3**: 113, 139–140
Franklin, Benjamin, **1**: 26; **2**: 96, 97
freemasonry, **2**: 265
Friendship, **1**: 19, 27, 274
frond. *See* leaf types
Fruitboys, **1**: 263, 264
Frutegirl, **1**: 264
game keeper, **1**: 26; **2**: 155
Ganymede, **1**: 14
gardener, **1**: 20, 26, 41, 44–85, 229, 274
Gardners. *See* gardener
Garrison Pottery, **1**: 28
Gasconian, **1**: 27, 161, 162
Gay, John, **2**: 129
George IV, King, **2**: 91
George, Saint, and the dragon, **1**: 26; **2**: 83, 84, 256
Girl and Lamb. *See* shepherdess
goat, **1**: 27; **3**: 141–144
Goethe, Johann Wolfgang von, **2**: 41
Good Girl, Good Boy, **1**: 103, 104

Grape Group, **1**: 43
figures by, **1**: 43, 63; **2**: 247
Gray Base Group, **1**: 41
figures by, **1**: 41, 67, 84, 223; **2**: 35–37, 190
Greatbatch, Thomas, **1**: 28
Grecian Daughter, 2:46
Green, John and Joshua, **1**: 14
Grimaldi, **2**: 56
Grocott, Samuel, **1**: 38
Gruitt, Thomas, **1**: 28
Guitar Player, **1**: 114
Hackwood, William, **2**: 120
hairdresser, **1**: 235–237
Hall, Ralph and John, **1**: 12
Hall, Samuel, **1**: 12, 13
figures by, **1**: 12, 64–66, 183, 187; **2**: 11–13, 54, 133, 145, 146, 179, 180, 189, 237; **3**: 9, 20, 50, 75, 97, 98, 155, 162, 163, 185–188 ,219, 225, 245, 246
Hamlet, **2**: 26
Handel, George, **1**: 27; **2**: 49
Hanshall, Thomas, **1**: 28; **2**: 135
hare, **2**: 150; **3**: 184
harlequin, **2**: 57, 58
Hartley, Greens, & Co., **1**: 14
Hartley, William, **1**: 14
Hay Maker, **1**: 26, 221
hedgehog, **3**: 179
Henderson, Thomas, **1**: 28
Herculaneum Pottery, **1**: 28
Hercules, **1**: 27
Hessian, **2**: 119
Hogarth, William, **2**: 50, 256
Home, John, **2**: 73
Homer, **1**: 22
Hood, George, **1**: 19, 38
Hooke, Theodore, **2**: 70
Hope, **1**: 18, 21, 24, 28; **2**: 183–194
horse, **3**: 145–147
horse with rider, **2**: 5–15
Hudibras, **1**: 26; **2**: 50–51
Humble, Richard, **1**: 15
hunter, **2**: 136–151
Hygeia, **1**: 24
I hope I don't intrude, **2**: 66
Iphigenia, **1**: 24, 27
It's quite hoptional, **2**: 68
Jarvis, Joseph, **1**: 28
Jennings, Henry Constantine, **3**: 108
Jeremiah, **2**: 202
Jervis, John. *See* Vincent, St.
Jesus, **2**: 161–166, 195–201
Jewish watch seller, **1**: 251
Jim Crow, **2**: 55
Jobson and Nell, **1**: 24, 28; **2**: 52–54
jockey, **2**: 14
John & Mary, **3**: 249
John the Baptist, **2**: 220
John, Saint, **1**: 27; **2**: 222–230
Jolly Traveller, **1**: 248
Josephine, Empress, **1**: 28
Jupiter, **1**: 27, 274
Kenney, James, **2**: 68
Kent factory, **2**: 129
King David, **1**: 26; **2**: 203
King, Tom, **2**: 78
Kirkaldy, **2**: 67; **3**: 144
Knottingley Pottery, **1**: 21
Lady, &, **1**: 27; **2**: 147
Lakin & Poole, **1**: 14, 31
figures by, **1**: 14; **2**: 49; **3**: 256
Lakin, Thomas, **1**: 14, 241
Lancret, Nicolas, **3**: 30
Land Lord, & Landlady, **1**: 240
Langan, Jack, **2**: 122, 124
Lazarus, raising of, **2**: 241, 215
Leaf Mat Group, **1**: 42
figures by, **1**: 42, 106, 268; **3**: 9, 41, 42, 49, 50, 96, 120, 208, 212, 254
leaf types, definitions, **1**: 6
Leather Leaf Group, **1**: 32, 33
figures by, **1**: 32, 46, 73, 92, 146, 150, 151, 224, 225, 232, 259; **2**: 8, 11, 147, 152, 165, 168, 169, 193, 211, 249, 250; **3**: 6, 41, 52, 77, 112, 155, 156, 203, 252
Leeds Pottery, **1**: 15
figures by, **1**: 15, 50, 211; **2**: 98; **3**: 145
Leek, Thomas, **1**: 28
leopard, **3**: 156, 158–160, 163, 166, 169–171
Liberty and Matrimony; **3**: 30–31
lion, **2**: 85–88; **3**: 148–168, 171–173, 259, 260
Liston, John, **2**: 62, 64, 65, 68–71
Little Jockey, **2**: 60
Log, Lubin, **1**: 17; **2**: 68, 69
London Cryers, **1**: 256
Lost Coin/Piece Found, **1**: 21, 26, 274; **2**: 204–207
Lost Sheep Found, **1**: 21, 26, 274; **2**: 206–211
Loyal Volunteer, **2**: 111, 117, 118
Lucy, Saint, **2**: 220
Luke, Saint, **2**: 222–230
Macbeth, Lady, **2**: 80
Madonna and child, **1**: 22, 24; **2**: 241–244
Malibrain, Maria, **2**: 61, 92
Marat, Jean-Paul, **3**: 256
Mark, Saint, **2**: 222–230
marmot girl, **1**: 21, 251, 252
Marten, Maria, **3**: 261–267
Mate, & Mate, **1**: 26, 51, 77–79, 160, 161, 222; **2**: 148
Matthew, Saint, **2**: 222–230
Maximus, Valerius, **2**: 46
McArdell, James, **2**: 28
Menagerie, **3**: 259
menagerie, **3**: 11–15
menagerie deaths; **3**: 259–260
Mercury, **1**: 7, 31
mermaid, **3**: 176, 177
Metcalf J., **3**: 145
milkmaid, **1**: 229–234
Milton (maker's mark), **1**: 28; **3**: 122
Milton, John, **1**: 27; **2**: 99, 103
Mind Dash, **3**: 123
Minerva, **1**: 14, 16, 27, 30
Molineaux, Thomas, **2**: 122–124
Moncrieff, William Thomas, **2**: 73, 79
monk, **1**: 24; **2**: 261, 262, 264
monkey, **3**: 182
Morris, J., **1**: 28; **2**: 127; **2**: 127
mouse, **3**: 39, 175
Mower, **1**: 26, 220, 222
Munro, Hugh, **3**: 257
musician, **1**: 25, 34, 38–41, 105–176
Mysore, **3**: 257
Napoleon. *See* Bonaparte
Neale & Co., **1**: 5, 15, 16, 22, 31, 210
figures by, **1**: 16, 154, 155, 208; **2**: 24
Neale, James. *See* Neale & Co.
Nell. *See* Jobson and Nell
Nelson, Horatio, **1**: 22, 28; **2**: 108
Neptune, **1**: 21, 26, 28, 30
Nero, **3**: 155
New Marriage Act, **1**: 29
Newton, Isaac, **1**: 27; **2**: 98
Nicodemus, **2**: 161
No! am I a gentleman?, **2**: 70
N. S. Dobom Despacho, **2**: 244
nun, **2**: 262, 263
O My Father..., **2**: 163
offering of Isaac, **2**: 156–160
old age, **1**: 24, 27, 274
Old Up If You Please, **3**: 9
Ophelia, **2**: 26, 27
owl, **3**: 20
Palmer, Humphrey, **1**: 15, 22
panther, **3**: 156
Parable of the Lost Coin. *See* Lost Coin
Parable of the Lost Sheep. *See* Lost Sheep
Parable of the Prodigal Son. **2**: 213
Parable of the Wise and Foolish Virgins. *See* virgin
parson and clerk, **2**: 256, 259. *See also* vicar and Moses
parson, **2**: 109
Partner, & Partner, **1**: 26, 27, 157, 251; **3**: 31
Pastime, **1**: 131, 134, 135
Patriotic Group, **1**: 34, 35
figures by, **1**: 34, 35, 45, 68, 83, 88, 89, 129, 130, 144, 145, 147–150, 167, 171, 172, 186, 188, 189, 225, 226, 229, 231, 234–237, 248, 258, 263, 264; **2**: 5–7, 19, 31, 113, 138, 157, 158, 161, 173, 174, 180, 181, 199, 202, 206, 210, 245, 246; **3**: 5–8, 47, 48, 58, 60, 61, 63, 64, 72, 73, 87–89, 115, 119, 133, 139, 143, 146, 156–159, 171, 172, 197, 208, 220, 226, 236, 242, 249, 250, 254, 255, 264
Paul, Saint, **1**: 20, 27; **2**: 231–233
Paulson, Joseph, **1**: 7
peacock, **3**: 19–25
pearlware, **1**: 5
Peasant Worshiping. See *Worshiper*
performing animals, **3**: 5–10
Pero. *See* Roman Charity,
Peter and the lame man, **2**: 214, 215, 239
Peter, Saint, **1**: 20, 27; **2**: 234–238
Phillip, Saint, **1**: 27; **2**:219
Phillips, Alexander, **1**: 28
Phillips, John, **1**: 28
Pidcock, Gilbert, **3**: 11
Pieta, **2**: 166
pig, **3**: 180
pigeon, **3**: 23
Pipe Player, **1**: 114
piper. *See* musician
Plant, Benjamin, **1**: 28
Plato, **1**: 22
Plenty, **1**: 22
pointer. *See* dog
Polito, Stephani, **3**: 11
Polito's Menagerie, **3**: 11–14
Polstead, **3**: 261–264
Pomona, **1**: 16
Poole, John Ellison, **1**: 14; **2**: 65, 71
Poor Laborer, **1**: 246
Poor Maria, **2**: 47, 48
Poor Soldier, **2**: 116
Pope, Robert, **1**: 18
Prepare to Meet thy God, **1**: 100; **2**: 265
press ganger, **2**: 115
price guide. *See* values
priest, **2**: 261, 262
Prudence, **1**: 16, 21, 22, 273
Prudent Mother, **1**: 24
Pry, Paul, **1**: 17; **2**: 65–67, 69
pugilist. *See* boxer
Purity, **1**: 21
puzzle jug, **2**: 23
rabbit, **3**: 183–184
raising of Lazarus. *See* Lazarus
ram. *See* sheep
Raphael, **2**: 213, 214
Raymond, George Frederick, **2**: 94
Reading Boy, **1**: 91
Reading Maid, **1**: 86, 87
reading, **1**: 18, 86–104; **2**: 148
Red Barn murder, **3**: 261–267
Rennie, James, **3**: 37
Return from Egypt, **2**: 195–201
Return, **2**: 111, 112
Rice, Thomas Dartmouth, **2**: 55

Rinaldo & Armida, **1**: 14; **2**: 49
Robinson Crusoe, **2**: 77
Rom and Dog, **1**: 185
Roman Charity, **2**: 183
Roran Lion, **3**: 150, 151, 257
Rover, **3**: 123
Rowlandson, Thomas, **2**: 31, 34, 111
royal arms, **2**:85–88
royal supporters, **1**: 36; **2**: 85–88
Rualer/Rural, **1**: 136
Rubens, Peter Paul, **2**: 46, 102
Rural Pastime, **1**: 27, 120, 130, 131, 274
S. Barbar. *See* Barbara
S. Joao. *See* John the Baptist
S. Luzia. *See* Lucy
S. Maneoel. *See* Emanuel
S. Sebasti. *See* Sebastian
sacrifice at Lystra, **2**: 213
Sadness, **1**: 21
sailor, **2**: 111–115
Sailor's Farewell, Sailor's Return, **2**: 111–113
Saint. *See* individual names
Salt, Ralph, **1**: 17
  figures by, **1**: 17, 59, 102, 103, 169, 181, 182, 196; **2**: 66, 68, 69, 144, 225, 226; **3**: 52, 68, 89–91, 105, 193, 210, 219, 225, 229
Samuel anointing David, **1**: 30; **2**: 214, 239–240
Sancta Maria Ora..., **2**: 244
Savoyard, **3**: 5–8
Scheemakers, Peter, **2**: 102
Scotsman, **1**: 244
Scottish east coast potteries, **1**: 175, 213, 243, 244; **2**: 67, 194, 264; **3**: 25, 65, 82, 144, 155, 180, 216
Scufffle, **1**: 27, 274
seasons, figures emblematic of, **1**: 28. *See also* Winter, Spring, Summer, Autumn
Seaton, John, **1**: 21
Sebastian, Saint, **1**: 22; **2**: 218, 220
Selina, **1**: 17
Selman, J. & W., **1**: 28
Senior, J. W & G. W., **1**: 14
setter. *See* dog
Shakespeare, William, **1**: 21, 27; **2**: 24, 26, 28, 99, 102–103
sheep, **1**: 12, 39, 42; **3**: 185–237
shepherd, **1**: 10, 11, 154, 177–219, 274
shepherdess, **1**: 30, 41, 177–219
Sheppard, Jack, **2**: 79
Sherratt Group, **1**: 36, 37
  figures by, **1**: 36, 37, 49, 51–54, 86–88, 100–102, 106–111, 137–139, 152, 165, 166, 181, 189–192, 203, 204, 238–240, 245, 256, 257, 268–271; **2**: 17, 31–33, 39, 40, 46, 55, 63, 66, 67, 75, 84, 86, 92, 118, 130–132, 137, 138, 151, 157, 162–164, 175, 176, 186–189, 198, 199, 223, 231, 235, 242, 261, 265; **3**: 5, 9, 11–15, 18, 26, 27, 41, 50, 51, 59, 62, 77, 80, 85, 106, 123, 127, 128, 132, 139, 150–153, 159, 160, 200–202, 213, 221, 222, 229–231, 240, 241, 248, 249, 255, 257–260. 262–267
shoemaker, **1**: 235–238
Shoemaker & Mate, **1**: 236
show man, show woman, **1**: 24, 169–175
Shrigley, Thomas, **1**: 14
Simon. *See* Cymon
slave, **2**: 120–121
Sloth, **1**: 247
Smith, Theophilus, **1**: 18, 21, 27
  figures by, **1**: 18, 211; **2**: 191
socket bocage. *See* bocage in socket
soldier, **2**: 111, 116, 117, 119
Songsters, **1**: 136, 175
Souter Johnny, **2**: 38–40
Spanish Dancer, **1**: 27, 163
Spanish Shepherd, **1**: 27, 209, 210
sphinx, **3**: 178
Spinning, **1**: 27, 244
sportsman, **1**: 24, 90; **2**: 136–151
Spring, figures emblematic of, **1**: 16. *See also* seasons
Spring, Thomas, **2**: 122, 124
squirrel, **3**: 238, 239
stag. *See* deer
Starred Anthemion Group, **1**: 43
  figures by, **1**: 43; **3**: 71, 96, 142, 209, 232
Stephan, Pierre, **1**: 28; **2**: 93, 105, 108
Sterne, Laurence, **2**: 47
Stevenson, Dale, & Godwin, **1**: 7
stoup, **2**: 167
Straw Flower Group, **1**: 42
  figures by, **1**: 42, 67, 194, 254; **3**: 51, 70
Summer, figures emblematic of, **1**: 16
Sunday school teacher, **1**: 244
Sunderland Pottery, **1**: 28
swan, **3**: 20
sweep. *See* chimney sweep
Swinton Pottery, **1**: 28; **3**: 85
Swipes, Sam, **1**: 24, 246; **2**: 70
Syntax. *See* Doctor Syntax
Tam O'Shanter, **2**: 38–41; **3**: 11
Tasso, Torquato, **2**: 49
Tee Total, **3**: 11
Tenderness, **1**: 27, 274
Thom, James, **2**: 38
Thomas and Annas, **3**: 249
Thompson, John, **1**: 21
tiger, **3**: 151, 157, 162, 163, 167, 259, 260. See also *Death of Munro*.
Time clipping the wings of love, **1**: 14
Tippoo's Tiger, **3**: 257
Tipu, **3**: 257
tithe pig, **1**: 43
Tittensor & Simpson, **1**: 18
Tittensor, Charles, **1**: 18
  figures by, **1**: 18, 80, 90, 268; **2**: 22; **3**: 54, 104, 135, 188
Tomlinson, Foster, Wedgwood & Co, **1**: 21
Tomlinson, William, **1**: 21
tortoise, **3**: 179
town crier, **1**: 245
tree grafter, **1**: 44, 45
triton, **1**: 22
Tunnicliffe, Michael, **1**: 38
Tunstall Group, **1**: 38–40
  figures by, **1**: 38–40, 48, 68–70, 128, 129, 143, 144, 172, 173,192, 193; **2**: 143, 179, 229; **3**: 48, 49, 71, 72, 86, 87, 204, 220, 221
Turk, **1**: 24; **2**: 16–23
turkey, **3**: 20
Turner, John and William, **1**: 28
Turpin, Dick, **2**: 78
tythe pig, **2**: 245–255
unicorn, **2**: 85–88
Urania, **1**: 14
Val Lay, **3**: 123
values, **1**: 6; **2**: 4; **3**: 4
Van Dunder, **1**: 22; **2**: 71, 72
Van Dyck, Anthony; **2**: 49, 102
Van Tromp, Cornelius, **1**: 26; **2**: 109, 110
Vanina, Peter, **1**: 28; **2**: 99, 102
vendor, **1**: 24, 249–272
Venus, **1**: 16, 21, 26–28, 30
Vestris, Eliza, **2**: 62–64, 69
vicar and Moses, **1**: 27, 274; **2**: 256–258
vicar, **3**: 256–260
Victoria, Queen, **2**: 61, 92
Village Girl, Village Boy, **1**: 96
Village Group, **1**: 30, 127, 128
Village Maid, **1**: 86
Village Songsters, **1**: 129
Vincent, Earl St., **1**: 28
Virgin Mary. *See* Madonna and child
virgin, wise, **2**: 212
Voltaire, **1**: 27
Voragine, Jacobus de, **2**: 83
Wallace, **3**: 155
Walton, John, **1**: 19, 20
  figures by, **1**: 19, 55, 56, 89, 90, 136, 168, 179, 180, 187, 188, 215, 216, 228, 249; **2**: 85, 87, 124, 146, 148–150, 166, 172, 192, 195, 196, 206, 224, 231, 234, 236; **3**: 10, 29, 36, 54, 55, 64, 98, 101, 117, 133, 148, 166, 184, 189, 190, 233, 234
Walton, Joshua, **1**: 19
Washington, George, **1**: 22
Water, figures emblematic of, **1**: 28, 29
Waters, Billy, **1**: 24; **2**: 73–75
water pump, girl at, **1**: 243
Wedgwood, John and Thomas, **1**: 25
Wedgwood, Josiah, **1**: 21, 22; **2**: 83
Wedgwood, Ralph, **1**: 21, 24
  figures by, **1**: 21, 212, 251; **2**: 25, 43, 44, 184, 185, 205, 209; **3**: 22, 148
Wesley, Rev. John, **2**: 261
Wellington, Duke of, **1**: 22; **2**: 105–107
whistle, **3**: 17, 18
Whitefield, Rev. George, **1**: 16
widow/*Widow of Sarepta*, **1**: 26, 27; **2**: 168–181
Wild Man & Bair, **3**: 7
Wilkes, John, **2**: 95
William III, King, **2**: 89, 90
Wilson, John and James, **1**: 15
Wilson, Robert and David, **1**: 15, 16
  figures by, **1**: 16
Winter, figures emblematic of, **1**: 16, 26. *See also* seasons
woman of Samaria, **2**:162
Wombwell, George, **3**: 11, 259
Wombwell's Menagerie, **3**: 11, 12, 14, 15, 259
Wood & Caldwell, **1**: 21, 22, 24
  marked figures by, **1**: 22, 273; **2**: 28, 29, 81, 82, 84; **3**: 46, 145, 165. *Also see* Wood, Enoch for unmarked figures
Wood, Enoch, **1**: 5, 21–25
  figures by **1**: 24, 70, 71, 82, 131, 140, 157, 158, 164, 165, 173, 174, 177, 184, 199, 200, 223, 227, 235, 250, 254–256, 260, 267, 273; **2**: 15, 19, 20, 24, 41, 53, 56, 59, 63, 67, 69, 70–73, 76, 89, 97, 99, 102, 103, 138–140, 166, 167, 185, 186, 209, 210, 220, 221, 230, 241, 244, 251, 261–263; **3**: 21, 22, 47, 56, 57, 60, 64, 67, 68, 75, 76, 98, 100, 108, 110, 111, 118, 124, 125, 136–138, 142, 143, 145, 148, 165, 166, 198–200, 216, 217, 234, 235, 237
Wood, Enoch Jr., Joseph, Edward, **1**: 22
Wood, John, **1**: 25; **2**: 109
Wood, Ralph II and III, **1**: 5, 18, 22
  figures by, **1**: 25, 75–79, 81, 82, 120, 130, 131, 153, 154, 156, 157, 162, 163, 166, 204, 209, 210, 217, 220–222, 244, 249, 251–253; **2**: 22, 23, 43, 50, 51, 83, 90, 94, 96–98, 100, 101, 109, 110, 117, 135, 147, 152, 155, 169, 184, 203–205, 207, 208, 218, 219, 230, 231, 234, 235, 241, 243, 256, 263, 264; **3**: 30, 31, 35, 44, 83, 113, 118, 132, 136, 139–141, 144, 145, 171, 203
Worshiper, **1**: 27; **2**: 263–264
Wright, Joseph, **2**: 47
York, Duke of, **1**: 28; **2**: 93
zebra, **2**: 5, 7, 11
Zingara, **1**: 27